Praise for *Embracing M*

MW00443628

"In these volatile, uncertain, complex, and ambiguous times (VUCA), we need to have a new way of leading. MESSY provides that leadership direction."

—**Andy Hargreaves**
research professor, Boston College
visiting professor, University of Ottawa, Canada
president and cofounder, ARC Education

"Through their coaching work with over 20,000 leaders worldwide, Gallagher and Connor have written a book that gets to the heart of the challenges of school leadership while they offer valuable insight into how those leaders can overcome their challenges."

—**Peter DeWitt**
author and *EdWeek* blogger

"*Embracing MESSY Leadership* gives vibrant life—purpose, meaning, and action—to a fresh and deeper understanding of the nature of leadership: leadership that can make a profound difference. Authors Gallagher and Connor convincingly anticipate the unfolding leadership landscape of schooling, placing the power of coaching at the heart of the urgent endeavour to lead education change."

—**Anthony Mackay**
board co-chair, National Center on Education
and the Economy, Washington, DC

"This is probably the most practical leadership toolkit that I have read in a long time. I would absolutely recommend it to all levels of school leaders."

—**Sir Mark Grundy**
chief executive, Shireland Collegiate Academy Trust, UK

"Easy to read, the leader stories and scenarios were very relatable. The strategies are practical and achievable for anyone. I would recommend it especially to aspiring and early career leaders but also leaders entering new environments that may be presenting previously unencountered challenges."

—**Angela Falkenberg**
president, Australian Primary Principals Association

"I have been advocating for the importance of school leaders who build relationships and not just relate. This book, *Embracing MESSY Leadership,* is absolutely needed, timely, and relevant in the ongoing leadership efforts in transforming schools."

—**Professor David Ng**
associate professor of policy, curriculum, and leadership,
National Institute of Education, Nanyang Technological University, Singapore

"This book is timely, relevant, and actionable for school system leaders as we strive to multiply our impact and empower others with whom we serve. I would absolutely recommend educational leaders at school and system levels read this book. Leaders who lead principals would find the coaching strategies highly applicable."

—**Valerie Truesdale**
senior assistant executive director,
AASA, The School Superintendents Association

"The best thing about this book is that it gives clear mental models, tools, and strategies, which school leaders can use to navigate their day-to-day work. I feel that the strategies and tools are quite applicable for the Indian context. One of the best things about this book is its brevity. It goes straight to the point and ensures every page has something new to offer to the reader. It is one condensed packet of wisdom that can only come from a vast experience of working with school leaders!"

—**Baidurya Bhusan Sen**
cofounder, Alokit India

"Leadership of schools might be 'messy,' but it does not need to be chaotic. It can be manageable, influential, and impactful. However, what makes an effective leader in the context of the complexity of today's schools is different than in the past. The key ideas in this book are very well 'cooked.' The authors have done the hard lifting, synthesising the latest in leadership thinking, illustrating this with succinct insights from coaches and leaders, and presenting ideas in ways that resonate and are accessible. The text reads as a conversation and, as a reader, I was made to feel that it was possible to learn new ways of being and doing, that I could take the ideas and use them. This felt like a gift."

—Robyn Baker
chairperson, Teaching Council of Aotearoa New Zealand

"*Embracing MESSY Leadership* honors the complexity of school leadership and the need for every leader to develop a set of adaptable skills to unlock the potential of themselves and their teams while being authentic. MESSY leadership draws on well-respected thought leaders and frameworks to reinforce their own organizational insights. Having coached over 20,000 leaders (within their organization), the authors have distilled the most common needs of school leaders and tools to address those needs for the leaders and their teams. You will likely find yourself in several of the case studies shared in the book and value the mindset shifts, applicable tools, and vivid context that can guide the way to meaningful, positive change."

—Lawrence Lee
executive director, School Leadership Alliance

"Gallagher and Connor shine a spotlight on the complex web of leadership and the coaching capabilities required to address familiar and unfamiliar problems in dynamic situations. Brimming with scenarios, tools, and frameworks, this book is timely for leaders committed to improving their own leadership capabilities and those they lead."

—Jenny Lewis
former executive director of ICSEI;
former CEO of Commonwealth Council for Educational Administration and Management

"Some of the things I liked most about the book included the solution-focused strategies that are shared and the scenarios that helped to illustrate each challenge. It caused me to reflect on areas that I consider my strengths and those I need to further develop and spend time thinking about how I can help develop these skills in the leaders I mentor. I think this book would serve as a wonderful text for educational leadership courses, mentor academies, and administrative professional learning communities."

—Kim Fry
professional learning coordinator,
Washington Association of School Administrators

"This book lit a fire under me that I had let exhaustion temper down. There were countless anecdotes that I could immediately relate to and numerous lessons that I could instantly apply to present challenges I face as a leader. Not only does the book point out the traps we can get into as a leader, but there are practical, readily applicable solutions to try out! This book is like taking all the best strategies that I'd been privy to over the years and condensing and bringing them all together to shape what leadership could and should reflect: MESSY but impactful. I would 100% recommend this book to others! I think leaders, from emerging to veteran, would find inspiration within each chapter."

—Vicki Bayer
deputy superintendent,
Green Bay Area Public School District, Wisconsin

"At Global School Leaders, we know that school leadership enables schools to thrive. But we also know that school leadership is difficult, complex, and often lonely. We are happy to see a book that recognizes this and is not afraid to name and talk about the messy nature of school leadership."

—Azad Oommen and Tamara Philip
cofounder and director of programs (respectively),
Global School Leaders

EMBRACING MESSY LEADERSHIP

Many ASCD members received
this book as a member benefit
upon its initial release.

Learn more at
www.ascd.org/memberbooks

ALYSSA GALLAGHER
& ROSIE CONNOR

EMBRACING MESSY LEADERSHIP

How The Experience of 20,000 School Leaders Can Transform You and Your School

ascd
Arlington, Virginia USA

bts spark
San Francisco • Toronto • London • Sydney

ascd

2800 Shirlington Rd., Suite 1001
Arlington, VA 22206 USA
Phone: 800-933-2723 or 703-578-9600
Website: www.ascd.org • Email: member@ascd.org
Author guidelines: www.ascd.org/write

bts spark

222 Kearny Street, Suite 1000
San Francisco, CA 94108 USA
Phone: 203-391-5222
Website: www.btsspark.org
Email: hello@btsspark.org

Richard Culatta, *Chief Executive Director;* Anthony Rebora, *Chief Content Officer;* Genny Ostertag, *Managing Director, Book Acquisitions and Editing;* Susan Hills, *Senior Acquisitions Editor;* Mary Beth Nielsen, *Director, Book Editing;* Jamie Greene, *Senior Editor;* Thomas Lytle, *Creative Director;* Donald Ely, *Art Director;* Lisa Hill, *Graphic Designer;* Circle Graphics, *Typesetter;* Kelly Marshall, *Production Manager;* Christopher Logan, *Senior Production Specialist;* Kathryn Oliver, *Creative Project Manager;* Shajuan Martin, *E-Publishing Specialist*

Copyright © 2024 BTS USA, Inc. All rights reserved. It is illegal to reproduce copies of this work in print or electronic format (including reproductions displayed on a secure intranet or stored in a retrieval system or other electronic storage device from which copies can be made or displayed) without the prior written permission of the publisher. By purchasing only authorized electronic or print editions and not participating in or encouraging piracy of copyrighted materials, you support the rights of authors and publishers. Readers who wish to reproduce or republish excerpts of this work in print or electronic format may do so for a small fee by contacting the Copyright Clearance Center (CCC), 222 Rosewood Dr., Danvers, MA 01923, USA (phone: 978-750-8400; fax: 978-646-8600; web: www.copyright.com). To inquire about site licensing options or any other reuse, contact ASCD Permissions at www.ascd.org/permissions or permissions@ascd.org. For a list of vendors authorized to license ASCD ebooks to institutions, see www.ascd.org/epubs. Send translation inquiries to translations@ascd.org.

ASCD® is a registered trademark of Association for Supervision and Curriculum Development. All other trademarks contained in this book are the property of, and reserved by, their respective owners, and are used for editorial and informational purposes only. No such use should be construed to imply sponsorship or endorsement of the book by the respective owners.

All web links in this book are correct as of the publication date below but may have become inactive or otherwise modified since that time. If you notice a deactivated or changed link, please email books@ascd.org with the words "Link Update" in the subject line. In your message, please specify the web link, the book title, and the page number on which the link appears.

PAPERBACK ISBN: 978-1-4166-3281-8 ASCD product #124011
PDF EBOOK ISBN: 978-1-4166-3282-5; see Books in Print for other formats.
Quantity discounts are available: email programteam@ascd.org or call 800-933-2723, ext. 5773, or 703-575-5773. For desk copies, go to www.ascd.org/deskcopy.

ASCD Member Book No. FY24-4 (May 2024 P). ASCD Member Books mail to Premium (P), Select (S), and Institutional Plus (I+) members on this schedule: Jan, PSI+; Feb, P; Apr, PSI+; May, P; Jul, PSI+; Aug, P; Sep, PSI+; Nov, PSI+; Dec, P. For current details on membership, see www.ascd.org/membership.

Library of Congress Cataloging-in-Publication Data

Names: Gallagher, Alyssa, author. | Connor, Rosie, author.
Title: Embracing MESSY leadership : how the experience of 20,000 school leaders can transform you and your school / Alyssa Gallagher & Rosie Connor.
Description: Arlington, Virginia : ASCD, 2024. | Includes bibliographical references and index.
Identifiers: LCCN 2023055220 (print) | LCCN 2023055221 (ebook) | ISBN 9781416632818 (paperback) | ISBN 9781416632825 (pdf)
Subjects: LCSH: Educational leadership. | School management and organization. | Educational change.
Classification: LCC LB2805 .G255 2024 (print) | LCC LB2805 (ebook) | DDC 371.2/011—dc23/eng/20240118
LC record available at https://lccn.loc.gov/2023055220
LC ebook record available at https://lccn.loc.gov/2023055221

30 29 28 27 26 25 24   1 2 3 4 5 6 7 8 9 10 11 12

EMBRACING MESSY LEADERSHIP

Foreword

Rebuilding education systems in a post-pandemic world is a process of collective transformation that will reimagine, reinvent, restructure—and improve—schools in ways we have never seen. As school leaders look for policies that will help them in this process, their role is entering a new spring, making proactive and visionary school leadership more important than ever. The transformation of education can start in everyday practice in schools, but it won't be easy, and it will require bold, innovative thinking about what school could be.

A clear, shared vision has always been central to successful school leadership, and now more than ever, leadership with a common purpose and shared direction is essential. Thankfully, this is the beating heart of Alyssa Gallagher and Rosie Connor's *Embracing MESSY Leadership.*

Two MESSY tools and strategies are worth highlighting here. The first is seizing momentum, which is about urging school leaders to be proactive and embrace new ways of thinking and working. Systemic change will likely continue to be slow and can't be taken for granted, so acting *now*, based on professional wisdom and expertise, is a critical part of effective leadership. The second is sensing the future, which requires leaders to think outside the box and ask questions such as "What could school be like?" Experimentation and innovation are the most promising tools to support leaders as they address daily challenges to school improvement. The ability to engage in this future-focused thinking with colleagues is another aspect of leadership that we need in a post-pandemic world.

Change is slow without significant mindset shifts. This is no less true in school settings. Coaching and leading educators within schools to create new elevated mindsets is a precondition to systemwide cultural transformation.

The book you hold in your hands is a guide to proactive, collaborative, and inclusive education in a world that continues to be characterized by uncertainty, growing inequalities, and disruption. It not only offers new ways to think about leadership in times such as this but also contributes to every school leader's practical toolbox to tackle everyday challenges. The MESSY leadership model identifies and delivers personalized advice about three key principles of school leadership.

First, school leaders should prioritize adaptability and flexibility to navigate uncertainties—especially in a post-pandemic world. The ability to swiftly adjust to changing circumstances, whether they are related to public health, technology, or educational policies, is crucial. This includes embracing hybrid learning models (i.e., combining in-person and online learning), accommodating diverse student expectations and needs, and being prepared for potential disruptions to teaching and learning. School leaders should also foster an educational culture that values innovation and continuous professional learning, encouraging teachers and staff to adapt their approaches in ways that best serve students who live in communities that are constantly evolving.

Second, leaders need to recognize and address the social and emotional impact of the COVID-19 pandemic. Importantly, they should prioritize the mental health and well-being of both students and staff. Indeed, implementing comprehensive preventive mental health programs, promoting work-life balance, and creating a supportive environment for open communication are essential. Demonstrating empathy in decision making and understanding the unique challenges faced by individuals within the school community also fosters a sense of belonging and resilience.

Third, it's essential to recognize that a heightened focus on equity and inclusion is now required in schools. School leaders must work together with their communities to eliminate educational inequalities that were exacerbated by or during the pandemic. This involves ensuring equitable access to technology, resources, and educational opportunities for all students. Furthermore, leaders should actively seek to address systemic inequalities with policymakers and their colleagues in other public sectors, engage with diverse perspectives, and create a learning environment that is inclusive and supportive of students from various backgrounds. Prioritizing equity in decision-making processes will contribute to a more just and resilient education system.

School leadership is key in addressing these principles in daily practice. Leading schools—and the diverse groups of people within them—is sometimes difficult, often imperfect, and always messy. Experienced school leaders know this and also understand the value of coaching and mentoring one another. Leadership, as research has shown, is a team sport, not an individual race for awards or recognition. The data behind this book also make this clear: Modern school leaders value and expect professional feedback, collegial empowerment and support, and a focus on the human side of school leadership.

—Pasi Sahlberg
professor of educational leadership,
University of Melbourne

Acknowledgments

We would like to express our gratitude to all those who have contributed to the creation of this book. *Embracing MESSY Leadership* is the result of a real team effort with many people involved throughout the process. Thank you to the regional heads of BTS Spark who shared in the thought leadership behind this book: Denise Barrows (United Kingdom), Maree Najem (Australia), and Sean Slade (North America).

We would also like to thank our broader BTS Spark team, including Spark Partners, program managers, and coaches. A special shout out to our incredible professional leadership coaches around the world who work directly with school leaders, coaching and supporting them to show up as the best version of themselves every day for their students and school communities.

Thank you to our MESSY Pioneers, a global group of education leaders across four continents who read, provided feedback on early drafts, and shared their experiences after trialing many of the strategies and tools included in this book. Their willingness to volunteer their time on top of already demanding leadership roles is greatly appreciated.

We are fortunate to be able to draw on the wisdom within BTS and over 1,000 leadership experts employed by BTS. The original MESSY leadership model and many of the tools in this book were developed by BTSers, in particular Jerry Connor.

Lastly, we would like to thank the leadership of BTS—especially Henrik Ekelund and Jessica Skon—for their incredible vision in creating BTS Spark to leverage the powerful BTS leadership tools and coaching expertise to support education leaders globally on a not-for-profit basis. We are all driven by a simple truth: Children deserve great leaders.

1

School Leadership Is MESSY . . . and School Leaders Know It!

School leadership is messy. If you are a school leader, you may have already felt this intuitively for a long time. Maybe you attended a leadership program or have a degree in educational leadership and were inspired by what you learned . . . and then found it really difficult to apply in practice. Maybe you start each term with high aspirations for how you intend to raise the quality of teaching and learning . . . only to find that each week is swallowed up by an endless list of "messy people issues" to deal with.

We hear your pain! We lead the not-for-profit initiative BTS Spark, and our coaches have supported more than 20,000 school leaders around the world. Coaching conversations offer an opportunity for school leaders to pause amidst the busyness of their everyday work and develop their leadership capabilities. Coaching also provides a space for leaders to reflect on their practice, talk through their toughest challenges, and identify new approaches.

We have witnessed the most amazing transformations. Our coaches help school leaders discover their own greatness. Along the way, they renew their sense of purpose, make breakthroughs in even the most broken working relationships, and find ways to collaboratively lead their school communities and improve the quality of education they provide to their students. Amazingly, 99 percent of all leaders who engage in coaching with BTS Spark report making a significant positive change in their leadership.

This book is grounded in the reality of leading schools: the lived experiences of thousands of school leaders—principals and team leaders—who have benefited from professional leadership coaching. If you have never been coached, then hopefully you will benefit from hearing others' stories (the quotes embedded in each of the chapters come directly from leaders being coached), learning some tricks of the trade, and using some practical strategies and tools our coaches use to support school leaders with their biggest issues.

> *"Knowing that other school leaders have the same challenges and have found solutions has been really affirming."*

What Are the Biggest Issues School Leaders Face?

School leadership can be a lonely business. When you're first promoted to lead a team or department, you may suddenly find yourself on your own. In previous roles, you likely had a network of colleagues you could talk to, sharing highs and lows, trading tips and resources, and so on. In the new role, though, you find yourself managing former peers (maybe even some of your friends) and the dynamic has fundamentally changed. Fast-forward a few years to when you're a principal, and you may feel lonelier still: in the spotlight, under pressure to be all things to all people, and unable to confide in anyone for fear of breaking confidentialities or appearing weak.

Another challenge is the complexity of working with adults, be they teachers, staff, parents, other school leaders, or colleagues in your school district. As one

school leader explained, “I feel so much more confident working with children. It’s what I was trained to do as a teacher. Adults are a whole different ballgame.”

This book synthesizes our research from coaching thousands of school leaders over a five-year period (2018–2022). Most of these leaders were based in North America, the United Kingdom, and Australia, but others were from a host of different countries, including Singapore, Kenya, South Africa, and Indonesia. They included school principals, assistant/deputy principals, department heads, instructional coaches, and some directors and superintendents. Even though their locations and job roles varied widely, the differences in their coaching needs did not vary as much as you might expect. Many of the challenges school leaders face are, indeed, universal.

When a school leader is talking with a coach, both understand that it’s a safe space and all conversations are confidential. This sense of safety and security typically allows school leaders to open up and speak their truths. At the outset, each school leader needs to agree with their coach on their key objective: the shift they would most like to make in their leadership. Usually, this is closely tied to a sticky challenge with which they are grappling.

Although every coaching conversation is one-to-one and personalized—and every school leader's context is unique—many face quite similar issues. Indeed, when we analyzed a sample of 1,700 school leaders' coaching objectives, we identified these nine common issues, ranked in order of frequency:

1. Giving feedback; having the courage to hold difficult conversations and hold others accountable.
2. Empowering and coaching others; not fixing others' problems; delegating and letting go.
3. Engaging others; getting buy-in; influencing others to change their practice.
4. Building confidence and personal authority; overcoming "imposter syndrome."
5. Slowing down; being less task-oriented; taking the time to be more people-oriented.
6. Getting things done; managing time; not procrastinating.
7. Attending to one's well-being and resilience; learning to say *no*; setting personal boundaries.
8. Seeing the bigger picture; prioritizing; taking the time to think strategically.
9. Creating a shared purpose; building a team vision; fostering greater collaboration.

Now imagine that you are embarking on a coaching journey and your coach asks you what your biggest win would be as an outcome of your coaching conversations. What would you name as your top issue? Is it one of the nine issues we identified or is it unique?

The Human Side of School Leadership

It's interesting to note that many of the top issues named by school leaders tap into their relational skills. Giving feedback, empowering others, getting buy-in, and building collaboration all require highly developed **inter**personal skills, and many others draw on our all-important **intra**personal skills (e.g., self-confidence, slowing down, managing your personal resilience).

Around half of all BTS Spark coaching conversations focus on supporting school leaders with relational leadership: widening their interpersonal skillset and strategies to handle complex interpersonal issues and work effectively with other teachers, school leaders, parents, and district colleagues. Around one-third of our coaching conversations focus on helping leaders develop their intra-personal skills: building their confidence, increasing their self-awareness, and deepening their emotional intelligence.

> *"I've had a lot of professional development in the past, but coaching has been like the missing piece in the puzzle for me. My coach helped me to work out how to support teachers and empower them. It's fundamentally changed the way that I work and lead."*

These priorities may not be a surprise to you. Nevertheless, they are rarely adequately reflected in leadership development programs offered to school leaders. Many courses continue to emphasize technical management skills (e.g., budgeting, human resources, health and safety), school improvement planning, and curriculum development. These are, of course, important, but we need to consider a "both and" approach here. It is unhelpful to expect school leaders to improvise their responses to scores of daily interpersonal challenges—especially since we know a silent majority of school principals globally have had little or no training for the job (Organisation for Economic Co-operation and Development, 2014).

We use the phrase *the human side of school leadership* to emphasize the importance of both interpersonal and intrapersonal skills that school leaders need to utilize (Slade & Gallagher, 2022). If you need further confirmation of this, look no further than the word cloud in Figure 1.1, which depicts the keywords that came out most strongly from our recent analysis of over 6,500 summary notes taken by coaches after their coaching conversations with school leaders.

FIGURE 1.1
Word Cloud Showing Most Common Keywords in Coaching Conversations

We do not intend to slide into the well-worn debate between instructional and transformational leadership; we believe this has been set up as a false dichotomy. It is a no-brainer that the quest to improve the quality of teaching and learning needs to serve as a north star to guide how school leaders spend their time, attention, and resources. Instructional leadership approaches can serve as helpful guides here. However, school leaders can only effectively drive change and improvement efforts by building capability and inspiring their teams, thus epitomizing the transformational leadership approach. What schools today urgently need is a combination of both instructional leadership and transformational leadership.

Recent research points to the importance of a combination of development strategies that include instructional, pedagogical, and transformational leadership to guarantee schoolwide success (Day et al., 2016). Great schools have great leaders who significantly influence and create improvements in teaching and learning, school culture, and the school's overall operation. All these improvements indirectly improve student learning outcomes.

Balancing the Me, Us, and It of School Leadership

What do we mean by the human side of school leadership? One model that helps many school leaders is super simple: the Me Us It model. Imagine three overlapping circles, where each circle represents an element of your work. The three circles are

It: This includes all the work you do as a school leader to provide a high-quality education for students and anything you do that improves teaching and learning, including activities such as teacher observation and evaluation, professional development, strategic planning, and budgeting.

Us: This includes all the relationships you have with stakeholders and the culture you want to create in your school in order to provide a high-quality education.

Me: This is the kind of leadership you need to model (and the personal shifts you may need to make) in order to achieve your goals for *it* and *us*.

Ideally, you want each element (*Me, Us, It*) to receive equal attention, but that is rarely how it plays out. As a school leader, you are probably continuously juggling all three without realizing it. That juggle is difficult, though, and many school leaders find that their time and attention is so overwhelmingly focused on *It*—putting student learning first, as it should be—that they neglect investing sufficient time in forging effective working relationships (i.e., *Us*) . . . and the *Me* component is often left behind completely!

> *"I know that I have to put on my own oxygen mask first so I can be effective for staff and students . . . but it's hard to do in practice."*

You Matter . . . Hugely

Does it matter if the *Me* takes a back seat? Surely, the student learning experience should be what it's all about? One could argue that the needs of the adults in a school—the needs of you and your colleagues—should take a back seat to students' needs, but is that sustainable?

Students' needs should be paramount. There's no arguing that. Still, students both need and deserve great leaders. If you're trying to make any changes to improve the quality of education that your students receive, then you're going to need buy-in from teachers, staff, parents, and the students themselves. Don't underestimate the importance of investing in the *Us*; it's essential to build the capability of colleagues, engage with stakeholders, and nurture the culture in your school that will support the changes you want to see.

Most importantly, don't neglect the ultimate truth: you matter enormously. Numerous studies point to the massive impact that the quality of school leadership has on the quality of education that students receive. Leithwood and colleagues (2008) famously cited school leadership as "second only to classroom teaching as an influence on pupil learning" (p. 28). This was qualified in a more recent article and the original claim revised: "School leadership has a significant effect on features of the school organization which positively influences the quality of teaching and learning. While moderate in size, this leadership effect is vital to the success of most school improvement efforts" (Leithwood et al., 2020, p. 6).

The Wallace Foundation analyzed data from 22,000 principals and made the startling finding that replacing an ineffective elementary school principal (rated at the 25th percentile for leadership effectiveness) with an effective elementary school principal (rated at the 75th percentile) produces average student gains across the entire school amounting to three months of learning in both math and reading (Grissom et al., 2021). Very simply stated, effective school leadership positively influences student achievement. You can debate how leadership effectiveness was ranked, but this does give pause for thought.

The MESSY Leadership Model

It's clear that school leaders matter, and it therefore pays dividends to invest in your leadership. In this book, we've crystallized the latest in leadership thinking and provide practical strategies and tools to strengthen your leadership capabilities. The original MESSY leadership model arose from work with leaders across all sectors (private, public, and not-for-profit). During the height of the COVID-19 pandemic, chief learning officers from more than 40 of the world's top organizations were interviewed to gain a better understanding of the types of leaders who were most successful at leading their organizations through a period of great uncertainty (Connor et al., 2020). Out of that work, the term *MESSY leadership* evolved to describe the surprising traits these leaders exhibited (Figure 1.2).

Once the notion of MESSY leadership was born, we found that the associated concepts gained strong traction among school leaders. Through numerous conference keynotes, we shared the key themes around MESSY leadership with school leaders at all levels and discovered that they not only loved having the so-called messiness of their jobs out in the open but also enjoyed being challenged with an aspirational model of leadership they could strive toward. All that was missing were practical strategies that would help them expand their leadership toolkit and make confident steps toward becoming MESSY leaders.

Our coaches of course do this—one conversation at a time. They draw on BTS Spark's expansive curriculum of 33 leadership mindsets and coach school leaders to unlock their potential, shift their mindsets, and embrace new approaches to strengthen their leadership practice. (More on this in Chapter 7.) This book attempts to share these insights, strategies, and tools with you.

FIGURE 1.2
The MESSY Leadership Model

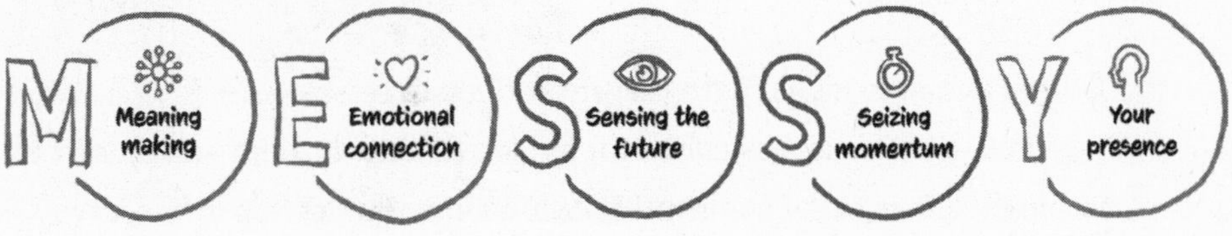

Your Journey to Becoming a MESSY Leader

Over the next five chapters, we will unpack the five key traits and mindsets of MESSY leadership. Adopting these specific mindsets will make it easier for you to lead in a complex world:

Meaning Making will help you create a shared vision and engage others (both staff and stakeholders) in this work by collaborating more effectively.

Emotional Connection will help you build deeper, more trusting working relationships to give feedback and hold difficult conversations where needed.

Sensing the Future will help you think outside the box and tackle entrenched school improvement problems through experimentation and innovation.

Seizing Momentum will help you be proactive, gain control of how you prioritize your time, and embrace new ways of working.

Your Presence will help you build your confidence as a leader, understand what holds you back, and learn how you can overcome this.

The final three chapters will then show how you can make a shift in your mindset to create a sustained shift in your leadership practice, along with strategies you can use to coach others on your team. This is what transformational leadership coaches do well, of course, but we will help you understand the principles behind mindset work and share some basic approaches to get you started.

There is no prize for reading every chapter in order. In fact, we encourage you to dip in and out of chapters as they feel relevant to your current leadership experience and journey. If you have a pressing need to address, why not fast-forward to the relevant chapter?

Each chapter includes

- A key challenge to identify the larger problem to be solved.
- A key idea that challenges conventional leadership wisdom and embraces new perspectives to get you thinking about your leadership differently.

- A detailed description of the relevant mindset shift so you can get a clear understanding of what it entails.
- A MESSY monitor, which encourages you to self-reflect on where your current leadership practice lies with respect to this aspect of MESSY leadership.
- Case studies that illustrate how other school leaders have embraced this new way of working, with support from our coaches. (All case studies are based on real school leaders we have coached, but various details have been changed to ensure total anonymity.)
- Insights from our amazing coaches around the world.
- Practical tools that provide scaffolds for integrating key MESSY concepts into your everyday conversations and leadership practice.
- Tips and "aha moments" from school leaders that relate helpful advice to understand new concepts and embrace new strategies. (You'll find many of these show up in sidebar quotes throughout the book.)
- Go-do actions that challenge you to immediately apply MESSY leadership tools and ideas in your everyday work.

Above all, we hope that this book will help you find a simple way to lead in today's complex world. We have worked with dozens of MESSY Pioneers—practicing school leaders across four continents who have embraced and trialed the MESSY leadership concepts—and been inspired by their efforts. As a result, we have woven many of their experiences into this book so it can serve as a practical handbook. For a printable toolkit of MESSY leadership resources to share with your team, go to btsspark.org/messyleadership.

We stand on the shoulders of giants: 20,000 school leaders who have engaged in coaching with us to strengthen their leadership, 300 coaches in 37 countries, and 1,000 leadership experts within our organization. With that kind of support, our job as authors was easy.

Schools need MESSY leaders. We wish you all the best in your efforts to become a MESSY leader.

2

M for Meaning Making

Key Challenge: How can I create a shared purpose and bring others along with me?

Uncommon Sense: It's more empowering for your team if you share leadership with them rather than trying to limit their workload.

Olivia was an assistant principal who had just been appointed as acting principal of a large suburban school. She had a passion for education and a clear vision of where she wanted the school to go, but was uncertain about how best to collaborate with everyone in the school to create a shared vision. Soon after assuming the principalship, Olivia observed some ineffective teaching practices in several classrooms, which prompted her to analyze student achievement data. Sure enough, the poor teaching practices she observed were contributing to poor student outcomes. In order to have a positive effect on the quality of education students received, Olivia knew she needed to challenge her staff, especially some of the more experienced teachers who had become complacent, and identify specific instructional practices in need of improvement.

Olivia was also concerned that her school needed to tackle issues concerning equity and access. The school had a high proportion of children with special needs (who each required an annual specialized instruction plan), but the process for getting these plans documented was extremely slow and inefficient. Therefore, Olivia began tackling individual issues and setting clear directions for improvement. She told her staff, "This is what I've noticed, here is how it is affecting students, and these are the steps we are going to take to improve."

As a new acting principal, it was tough work to take a stand, especially with such a senior staff. She was proud of her clarity and commitment to improving education outcomes for students, but two months after setting very clear directives, she realized that no one was following her. The whole experience reminded her of a quote by John Maxwell: "If you think you're leading but no one is following, then you are only taking a walk."

> *"I need to shift from fighting fires to lighting fires where other people gather."*

This felt like a particularly harsh description that didn't accurately capture all the work Olivia had done, but she couldn't deny the fact that, despite her best efforts, she simply was not having the impact she desired. As a new principal, Olivia was given the support of a leadership coach. During one emotional coaching session, her coach asked, "How are you *really* feeling?" Truth be told, Olivia felt devastated, exhausted, and isolated.

She responded, "I can see just by talking things through that I have taken too much on in isolation. I see now that I can be the spark to ignite change, but I can't be the one to keep the fire burning all the time."

Olivia had a few big aha moments during her coaching. She realized that she had clarity of vision guiding her work, but she hadn't involved her team enough in that vision. She also saw that she had been making many assumptions about her team, especially her assistant principals. The two assistant principals in the school, whom Olivia leaned on heavily, agreed with her school improvement priorities when she was around, but they undermined her work elsewhere. Given their years of experience, Olivia assumed they were capable of leading initiatives, but she quickly realized they required additional support and scaffolding to help lead change. She also recognized that she hadn't ever taken the time to look at things from their perspectives, which resulted in their minimal investment in doing "her work" or the work she was directing. All these insights presented leadership growth opportunities for Olivia.

With support from her coach, Olivia began to shift her leadership practices. She spent time co-creating a shared vision with her broader team and involved her assistant principals in the process much more, continually asking for their improvement ideas. She then delegated responsibilities, provided support, and held those individuals accountable for their results. She also deliberately made time for the many teachers who were ready and open to change—the early adopters. Instead of focusing all her energy on those who were resistant to change, Olivia began to engage and empower other key influencers within the school, creating a bigger ripple impact. After making these changes, she no longer had to do all the influencing or overrely on her assistant principals.

> *"To achieve the goal of 'leaving in the night without being noticed,' I need to ensure the organization is replicable and sustainable in my absence. Which requires a shift from me being the driver and key to improvement to seeing others as the drivers and the key to improvement."*

Olivia's experience is all too common. After thousands of coaching sessions around the world, we've learned that effectively engaging others from visioning through implementation of strategic initiatives is a real area of need. Too many leaders feel that they must do everything themselves—that the success of their school, their teachers, and even their students all hinges on them. However, the best leaders realize they cannot fix every problem themselves or be the sole owner of the future vision of the school. Doing so will likely mean they are headed down a path to burnout. Leaders are much more effective when they engage others in meaning making and creating that future. Just as teachers help students make personal connections to their learning, the most effective leaders focus on meaning making for their teams, helping them make sense of the knowledge, experiences, and relationships critical to their work. They are not only happier in their work but also more effective and able to achieve a greater impact.

Meaning making involves a shift from a mindset of "I care about providing students with a high-quality education so I work hard at what I do" to a more inclusive mindset of "I create a sense of shared agency and engage others in an inspiring vision."

How MESSY Are You?

Before diving further into meaning making, take a few minutes to reflect on your own leadership. How would you rate yourself on the different aspects of the Meaning Making MESSY Monitor (Figure 2.1)? Respond honestly, using the results as a baseline for your current leadership practices. Are you guilty of working in isolation, or do you use strategies to get the best of yourself and your team? If you want to level up and accelerate your leadership development, invite a critical friend to provide feedback. Friends and colleagues can often help us see our blind side and make us more aware of our impact on others. (An aggregate rubric, which combines each chapter's MESSY leadership monitor, can be found in Appendix A.)

If you found yourself selecting *Frequently* or *Very Often*, then these are likely areas of strength for you. However, if you found yourself selecting *Never* or *Rarely* on some of the items, then these are probably areas of struggle for you. The strategies and tools (Rubber Band, See Hear Speak, Presence Triangle)

FIGURE 2.1
Meaning Making MESSY Monitor

Meaning Making Behaviors	Never	Rarely	Sometimes	Frequently	Very Often
My work is driven by a clear sense of purpose.					
I am confident while co-creating a vision with others.					
When leading change, I listen to what others have to say and am open to shifting my own point of view.					
I demonstrate empathy by stepping into another person's shoes to try and feel what they are feeling.					
I can collaborate effectively in a team setting.					
I empower my team to take ownership and accountability.					
I am comfortable letting go and trusting others.					

shared in this chapter are designed to support you in building your leadership capabilities to better make meaning with your team.

More and more education leaders are beginning to recognize that, given the conditions they face and the vast amount of work to be done, they cannot do everything to achieve the vision they have for their school or department—and they certainly cannot do it alone. This isn't an easy leadership shift to make as it requires leaders to switch from holding the reins tightly—trying to create a vision and then personally ensure all initiatives are a success—to loosening the reins, maybe even letting go completely and trusting that others will succeed. Successful leaders find a balance between inspiring stakeholders, intentionally creating space for collaboration, and empowering their team not only to solve problems but also to fully own and be accountable for the work to be done. When leaders strike this balance, those on their team find their work much more meaningful since they see their individual efforts as part of the broader vision and feel a sense of shared purpose.

This is not an easy leadership shift to make, but it is a shift that is supported by research. Collaborative leaders don't just make others feel included, they increase the self-efficacy of staff (0.92 effect size) and build collective teacher efficacy (1.57 effect size) (Hattie, 2008). As John Hattie has correctly pointed out, a school staff that believes it can collectively accomplish great things very likely will. Peter DeWitt (2016) expands on Hattie's research and unpacks six leadership factors in his book on collaborative leadership, highlighting the importance of collective efficacy. In short, when teachers believe they can make a difference and positively influence students, they are more likely to do so. Likewise, Michael Fullan (2018) identifies joint determination as one of three key habits for nuanced leadership and collaboration as one of six global competencies. There is real power and potential impact for leaders who can effectively make meaning and collaboratively connect their team to a shared vision.

Reconnecting to Your *Why*

We know firsthand that leaders want to have a positive impact, yet we also know it can be a challenge to stay connected to your purpose as you move further from the classroom into leadership positions. Kudos to you if you still feel connected to your *why* and purpose, but if you are like many leaders and your *why* feels fuzzy, try spending a few minutes reconnecting to your purpose. This doesn't have to be a huge undertaking. You can do this easily by asking yourself a few reflective questions. You may want to craft questions unique to your situation, but below are a few to get you started:

- What difference do I want to make for our students?
- What are my top priorities in leading my school and am I focusing my time and energy on them effectively?

- How am I prioritizing my own personal and professional development?
- What steps can I take to continue growing as a leader?
- Why do I believe that our school can create a lasting, positive change?
- Why do I want to lead our school to achieve our mission and purpose?

Reflecting on questions like these helps you gain greater clarity, purpose, and intention in your leadership, leading to more effective and meaningful outcomes. These prompts contain a mix of *what, how,* and *why* questions. If you are clear on your vision and purpose, then you are ready to spend more time on the *how* (the process or methods you use to achieve goals) and *what* (the programs, curriculum, or experience you want to provide students). If you are feeling fuzzy about your vision, start with *why* questions.

The idea of starting with *why* comes from Simon Sinek's The Golden Circle, which consists of three concentric circles: *why* at the center, *how* in the middle, and *what* on the outside (Sinek, 2011). Sinek believes that leaders are most successful when they have a strong *why*—the purpose, beliefs, or values that drive them. Reconnecting with your own purpose can help you think differently about your team through a purpose-led lens.

Creating a Vision

Once you've reconnected with your *why*, what's the next step? Many leaders, like Olivia, have ideas about the future vision for their school but may struggle to involve others in their vision. It's a fine line. Leaders feel like they must chart the course ahead, but at the same time they also know there must be shared ownership of the vision. In Olivia's case, it became clear that her colleagues didn't feel engaged in "her vision" and she belatedly realized she was only taking a walk with nobody following her lead.

A clear shared vision is important because it has the power to give your team energy to start and momentum to move forward. To have a great vision, you need to focus your energy on defining and working toward a future state rather than focusing on simply achieving tasks or objectives. It's a shift from allowing others to define your priorities to shaping the future you want for yourself, your school, and your community.

Imagine a rubber band that is stretched between two extremes. At one end is the current reality: an honest, open, and shared version of how things really are. At the other end is the vision: an exciting sense of the future and untapped possibility. (See Figure 2.2.) This analogy is used to describe the tension between a person's current reality, their desired vision, and the gap between the two (Fritz, 2014). That gap often creates a healthy tension, like the tension in a stretched rubber band, as people feel both pulled toward the desired outcome and held back by the constraints of the current reality. However, that tension can also be uncomfortable, and there is often a natural tendency to return to a familiar and comfortable state (i.e., a relaxed rubber band). By maintaining the tension and taking intentional action, individuals can stretch the rubber band and bridge the gap between their current reality and their desired outcome. This tension is both healthy and necessary; it provokes energy and momentum for the vision. If the current reality and vision are too close together, there is little or no energy in the tension. On the other hand, if the current reality and vision are too far apart—if the vision is unreachable and commitment is lost—then the rubber band snaps, and all the potential energy that was built up is lost.

FIGURE 2.2
The Rubber Band Model

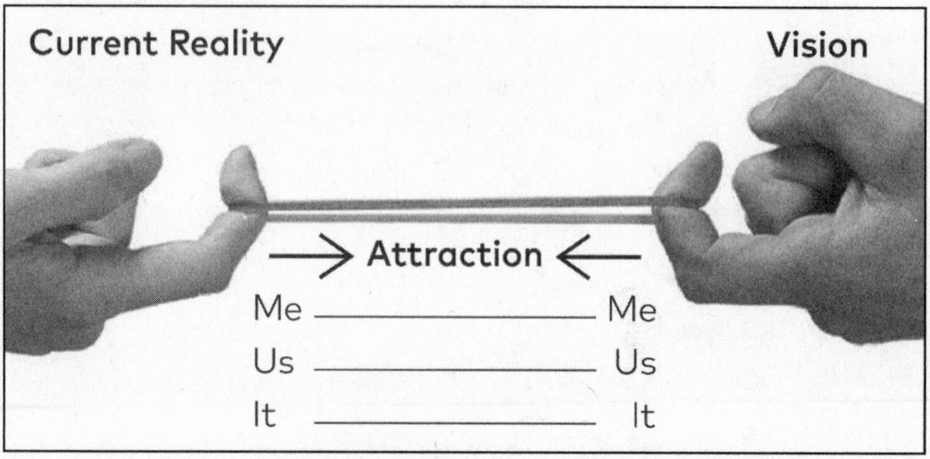

As important as it is to find the right tension between the current reality and future vision, it is imperative that the vision incorporates the Me Us It model (shared in Chapter 1), which can be layered on top of the rubber band model. When this is done, the vision is better set up to generate excitement and be easily communicated and understood. Try mapping your current reality and future vision against all three components of Me Us It.

It encapsulates the work necessary to make changes. Can you ground your vision in an honest view of reality so you and your team are clear on what needs to change? How does this contrast with your vision for an improved education for your students: the change you are working toward and the impact you aim to have?

Moving on to *Us*, what do you notice about your collective team and your relationships with them? What might they need to do differently to achieve the vision, which relationships might you need to invest in, and what culture do you want to create?

Don't forget about *Me*! Leaders often talk about what they want to change and how it will affect the collective whole, but many forget to consider how they need to change to achieve that vision. This oversight means you lose the biggest lever for change you have: *yourself*! Therefore, try to answer the following questions. What is your current reality? How do you spend your time? Where is your energy spent? How might you need to step up your leadership to achieve the vision? Starting with yourself is important because you set an example for others. If you are not making personal changes to achieve your vision, how can you expect others to do the same?

Let's look at how Olivia used this model to find greater focus in her vision as she worked to implement strategic initiatives (Figure 2.3).

FIGURE 2.3
Olivia's Me Us It Model

Current Reality	Vision
Me: • Spending my time on daily tasks. • Overfocused on policy and procedures. • Occasional visits to classrooms but no real meaningful dialogue about vision or change.	**Me:** • Become a catalyst for change. • Spend short bursts of energy on the ground, working to launch key initiatives.
Us: • Teachers are working hard. • Teachers don't feel they can add anything to their plate.	**Us:** • Break down the fears and concerns so implementing change is seamless and effective.
It: • The new initiative is designed to address the needs of students in today's learning climate.	**It:** • Build a community of ambitious, dynamic, and forward-thinking educators focused on student success.

This model is a great framework to work through with your team. It will help you create a better understanding of the gap between your current reality and your shared vision. Once you craft your own vision, assess its effectiveness by asking yourself the following questions:

- Is there a balance of *Me, Us,* and *It*?
- Is everyone clear on their current reality? Are they clear on the change they need to make?
- Do we have the right amount of stretch between our current reality and future vision?

When you feel like you have a robust vision, it's time to think about how you can effectively engage others in this work so it doesn't all rest on your shoulders.

Creating the Conditions for Meaning Making

Leaders who focus on meaning making work hard to engage others in their vision, collaboratively building a shared purpose. Collaboration doesn't just naturally happen; in fact, traditional education structures may limit collaboration as they often unknowingly reinforce a separation between leaders and teachers, district office staff, and school staff. There are many practices and rules, both written and unwritten, that govern how schools operate, and many of these exist outside a leader's sphere of influence and may detract from their ability to collectively work toward a shared vision.

Given this context, school leaders must actively create the space and conditions for others to share their perspectives, including concerns and frustrations. Amy Edmondson, an organizational behavioral scientist from Harvard, first introduced the idea of team psychological safety and defined it as "a shared belief held by members of a team that the team is safe for interpersonal risk taking" (Edmondson, 1999, p. 352). Psychological safety helps create an environment in which everyone on the team feels free to contribute without fear of retribution or retaliation. In a psychologically safe environment, everyone, regardless of role or position, feels free to speak up with ideas, questions, concerns, or mistakes.

A cornerstone of psychological safety is vulnerability, especially as demonstrated by leaders. When leaders demonstrate vulnerability, it can permeate the culture of the entire school. Vulnerability may feel like a major obstacle, but it is best demonstrated in small moments of leadership—moments between individuals. Collectively, small moments of leadership add up to a broader shift that helps make meaning of the work we do. See Hear Speak and the Presence Triangle (see following sections) are two tools that can help leaders create more effective moments, conversations, and relationships that contribute to a school or district's culture.

Some aspects of these tools may feel familiar. In fact, one of our coaches noted, "I find that adults working in schools already know many of the strategies that we teach in coaching, and they even utilize them daily with students, but for some reason they forget that these same strategies work with the adults on their teams. They put them in a separate box and forget about them." If you, too, are guilty of this, then now is your chance to put these strategies into practice in your own leadership.

Building Rapport and Collaborating: See Hear Speak

To achieve a school's vision, school leaders at all levels must engage with, influence, and relate to all different types of people (e.g., students, parents, teachers, district colleagues, board members). Many of these connections and relationships develop easily and are positive in nature, but what happens when you don't naturally connect with others? How do you connect when you find someone difficult or challenging?

See Hear Speak (Figure 2.4) is a useful model that helps ground all relationships in empathy. On the surface, empathy is a simple concept, yet we all have

FIGURE 2.4
See Hear Speak Model

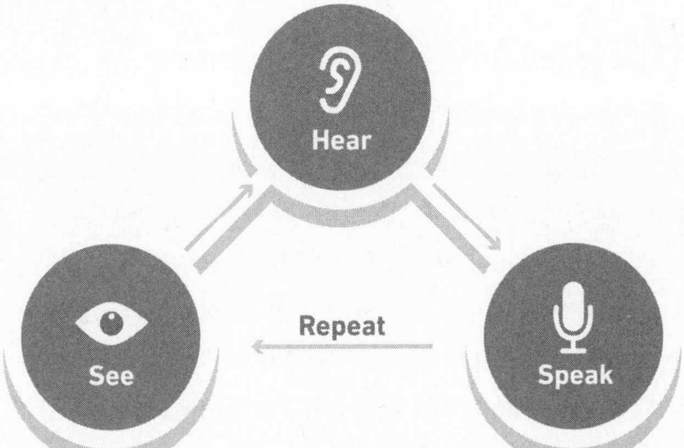

room to improve our empathy skills. Empathy is all about seeing others and helping them feel seen and express themselves more fully. It's also about speaking authentically and sharing your true self. The strategies embedded in See Hear Speak are likely ones you already know and intuitively use. However, without focus and clear intention, they can be easily forgotten in the hustle and bustle of leading schools.

Think back to the last time you were at a social gathering, an education conference, or any group event where you had to network and mingle with a variety of people. What was the experience like for you? Whom did you connect with? What conversations did you have? Hopefully, you felt seen, heard, and able to speak openly, but we've all been to group events where that wasn't the case. Likely, you experienced lopsided conversations—ones where either you did most of the talking or the other person did. This is partly due to human nature. Instinctually, the first thing we do when engaging with other people is speak. We focus on getting our message across rather than tuning into the other person and listening.

> *"See Hear Speak reminds me of the analogy that we have two eyes, two ears, and only one mouth, but we use the latter far more than we should!"*

The skill of empathy is to create moments when we truly see others, hear their voices, and openly discuss meaningful topics with them. Great leaders can create these moments in all sorts of contexts, even in crowded conference events and parties! The next time you find yourself in one of these situations or just really want to engage someone, consider the following See Hear Speak steps.

See: Try to see the person. Notice their preferences, speaking patterns, and behaviors, and mirror them if appropriate. Mirroring simple behaviors such as speech patterns or body language sets people at ease, as people are generally more positively inclined toward those they perceive to be like them. Check that they are comfortable with the location and timing of the conversation and consider what (if any) small talk may relax them. Acknowledgment works well to build rapport. For example, say, "Your lessons have been really engaging. Where are you getting your inspiration?" or "You seem a little more stressed than usual. Do you have a lot going on?"

Hear: Once the other person feels seen, they should visibly relax. Now is the time to hear what they have to say. Demonstrate committed listening by repeating a summary of what the other person says, deliberately using their own words as much as possible. Then give the other person an opportunity to agree with or modify your summary. As simple as it sounds, the benefits are enormous. Through this act, you're demonstrating active listening, clarifying and eliminating the opportunity for misalignment, and giving yourself an opportunity to digest their ideas before immediately responding. As Olivia worked to really hear people on her team, she reflected, "When I'm not at my best as a leader, I am not listening. I am in a telling space. I am going to pay more attention to this so I can embrace the way I want to be as a natural collaborator."

Speak: Once you've seen and heard the other person, you can share what you have to say. If possible, explicitly link your own ideas to the concerns and ideas you heard the other person express. Be concise, avoid opinions and judgments, and clearly assert what you want and need. After you've had the opportunity to speak, cycle back to the first step (see) and be observant about how your message has been received. It may help you realize that a message you shared didn't land well and give you an opportunity to clarify. For example, you could say, "You look upset with what I just said . . ."

Although these strategies are straightforward, getting the order right is often the hardest thing for most people to do. The next time you engage with another person, make the conscious effort to see first, hear second, and speak last. (Chapter 3 provides some additional speaking strategies, especially with respect to giving feedback to others.)

With a little effort and practice, See Hear Speak can become your norm and improve your ability to engage with anyone, regardless of your previous connection level. It's a simple yet powerful tool to help you foster greater collaboration and set the right environment for meaning making. Upon reflection, Olivia shared that she made a conscious effort to use the See Hear Speak model with her two assistant principals: "I made deliberate use of See Hear Speak when working with my two APs—reminding myself to look before rushing in and then to listen actively. I can see now they were rushing our conversations as they were concerned there was a lot to get through in limited time, but when they saw that I was determined not to rush, they both visibly relaxed and our conversations improved. Taking more time for these conversations led to more meaningful discussions about our work and achieving our vision."

Broaching More Challenging Relationships: The Presence Triangle

Meaning making can be especially challenging when you need to work with people who see the world very differently than you do. You may find some work relationships to be unusually stressful and energy-depleting, especially when there are conflicts. Nevertheless, it is possible to achieve breakthroughs in more difficult relationships—with students' parents, teachers, colleagues, or even family members—using the Presence Triangle.

Have you ever noticed that it is far easier to see both sides of someone else's argument when you're not an active part of the conversation? This is because you have some distance. This notion of distance can be used to improve your ability to see the context of any relationship. Take a moment to think about a relationship that makes you feel depleted. With that relationship in mind, you can use the Presence Triangle (Figure 2.5) to observe relationship dynamics, build empathy, and choose your next steps.

The Presence Triangle highlights three aspects of relationship dynamics: self, others, and conditions. The amount of trust, connection, and safety between individuals is dependent on the strength of the relationship, which can be strengthened using the Presence Triangle. Working your way through this model is most powerful when you can physically move through the process. If you have the room, set up two chairs facing each other and a third chair to the

FIGURE 2.5
The Presence Triangle

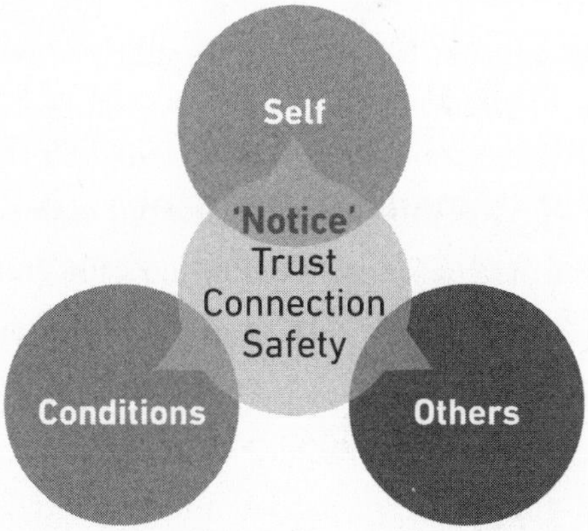

side. If you don't have room, you can mimic the physicality of this exercise by shifting your positions.

Self: Explore Your Mindset

Sit in your chair and think of a person with whom you're currently having difficulty or not seeing eye-to-eye. Call that person to mind. If it's easier, you can close your eyes and imagine them sitting in the opposite chair. When you look at the other person, ask yourself, "What do I see? What do I feel? What assumptions and beliefs do I have about this person?" Since you are alone, this is not the time to regulate or judge your thoughts. The more honest you are with yourself, the more insight you will gain.

Others: Explore Their Mindset

Now sit in the opposite chair as if you are the other person (or shift positions in your chair if you're only using one). Step into their proverbial shoes and mimic their usual posture. Imagine you are them—inside their body, wearing their clothes, living their life, and looking back at yourself. Ask yourself the same questions, but this time from the perspective of the other person, "What do I see? What do I feel? What assumptions and beliefs do I have about the other person?"

Conditions: Be an Outside Observer

Now move to the third chair off to the side and imagine you can look at both yourself and the other person. From this perspective, ask yourself, "What do I notice about these two people? What might be helpful for this relationship?"

Self: Return to Your (Expanded) Mindset

Finally, return to the original chair. What new insight or understanding do you have now that you didn't have before? What actions do you want to take as a result?

This simple reflection process can help improve relationships because it is grounded in empathy—for the other person, for yourself, and for the situation. The Presence Triangle guides us in how we can be proactive and shift the relationship dynamic, and it is much more effective than trying to "fix" the other person. The more we're able to see from another person's point of view, the more we can appreciate what's driving their behavior—and, therefore, understand how best to influence them.

This is the tool that helped Olivia reframe her relationship with her two assistant principals. When Olivia stepped into their shoes and looked back at herself, she saw her leadership through their eyes. She saw a leader who was rushed, working alone and dismissive at times. When she stepped into the role of impartial observer and viewed the relationship between her and the assistant principals, she could see why there were miscommunications and misunderstandings. As a result, she made the conscious choice to slow down and allow for more time in their weekly meetings.

These two strategies (See Hear Speak and the Presence Triangle) when practiced regularly will help you create more space—both literally and metaphorically—for others on your team to contribute and make meaning of your collective work. You're also likely to find yourself talking less, listening more, and observing more. School leaders who successfully align their practices with these strategies are surprised by how much their team engages and wants to fully participate. Most people in organizations are underutilized, yet they want to be fully utilized, and their capability can be leveraged with the right kind of leadership (Wiseman, 2017). Using these strategies also helps create high levels of trust in you and your leadership, which in turn helps staff be more likely to engage in change—even before they fully understand the plan. Gaining and building trust creates the organizational ability to move fast and adapt quickly.

Leading Change

What is your orientation to change? For many people, just thinking about change, let alone *leading* change, makes them uncomfortable. We are emotional beings that are sometimes rational, but our reactions to change are often primitive, learned, and temporary. We know it is not easy to change. Even if something isn't really working, we're much more likely to adapt rather than make a change. School start times provide a great example. We've known for at least a decade that adolescents aren't getting enough sleep. Research points to the benefits of a later school day for adolescents, yet the thought of shifting school start times is almost impossible for people to accept. What about parents who drop their kids off before work? What will this mean for parents with children in multiple schools? What about sports, traffic, and so on? All the "what ifs" get in the way, making it much more likely for people to just accept the status quo, even if it isn't ideal, rather than risk making a change.

Nevertheless, change is necessary. Change is continuous and the source of new opportunities, innovation, and growth. Leaders with a positive orientation to change do things differently because they see things differently. They create the conditions for their team to succeed in change and help them overcome resistance to change.

Confidently navigating through change is an important part of leadership that is often lost in the chaos of our day-to-day working lives. Once you've created a vision for change, it takes a lot of work to inspire those around you to achieve an effective transformation. Take a moment to think about your vision. What is a change you know you need to make? What is stopping you from making it? What might be stopping other people? As you dig into a change you want to make, it's important to remember that change is ultimately all about people. It's about taking advantage of their best thinking and mobilizing them to take action. Change is not just about you; it's about bringing everyone along with you.

When it comes to change, people tend to fall into two different groups—change champions and people less excited about change. Change champions are people who help make change happen: team members, colleagues, teachers, and mentors. They are the source of whatever change you want to see. They act as resources to help ensure your stakeholders adopt change. The broader group of stakeholders may be less excited about or motivated to change. Both groups are important, but in your work as a school leader, you'll have the most direct influence over the change champions.

Why do people resist change? How can you overcome that resistance? For the most part, people are wired to prefer stability and predictability. By its very nature, change brings about uncertainty, which causes confusion and destabilizes people's sense of security. Even though people may like the notion of change when it's talked about in the abstract or in the distant future, they get uncomfortable when that talk starts to hit close to home. Knowing that resistance to change is natural, you can choose to view this response as a starting point to explore and invite people to join the change conversation even if they are resistant. The formula for change describes the conditions necessary for change to occur:

$$D \times V \times F > R$$

D	V	F	R
Dissatisfaction with the status quo	Clear, compelling, and shared **vision**	The **first steps** toward action and creating momentum	**Resistance** to change

1. **Dissatisfaction** with the status quo: People need to understand and feel why the status quo is no longer acceptable. This is about a specific

dissatisfaction with the way things are today, not just a general mood of "dissatisfaction."

2. Clear, compelling, and shared **vision**: People need a vision for where the proposed change will take them. They need a picture of where they are collectively headed.
3. The **first steps** toward acting and creating momentum: Even with dissatisfaction and a clear vision, people can still have that notorious "deer in the headlights" reaction. For change to be successful, everyone needs clarity on what they should start doing, stop doing, and keep doing.

This change formula implies that all three elements must be present for change to occur. If they are, the combination of the three is greater than people's natural resistance to change. If any element is missing, then the product of the multiplication will be zero and thus not be greater than the resistance. Without all three, sustainable change will not happen. The beauty of this formula is that it can be used both at an individual level and at an organizational level. Try it! Think about a personal change you want to make and see if you have all the necessary elements. Our guess is that if you haven't been successful in making the change, it is likely because you are missing one of the critical elements.

In working with education leaders, we have found that most leaders have one or two of the necessary elements but are missing the third. The most missed element in education is dissatisfaction with the status quo. Education leaders may like to talk about the need for change, but in many cases, the current ways of working suit many educators just fine and they may not feel a compelling need to change. If this is the case, you may need to help generate more dissatisfaction with whatever problem you are trying to solve. This is exactly what Olivia discovered in her change efforts. She had made great strides in co-creating a vision and had identified some first steps, but there wasn't a dissatisfaction with the status quo. Teachers had accepted inequities in services for special education students and weren't concerned enough about student outcomes. In response, Olivia used a data-driven approach to increase the dissatisfaction.

Lighting Fires That Inspire

Throughout this chapter, we explored what it takes to be a MESSY leader who engages collaboratively with others for meaning making—shifting from fighting fires to lighting fires where other people gather.

The Me Us It, See Hear Speak, Presence Triangle, and change formula strategies are powerful tools to add to your leadership toolkit. School leaders who have implemented these strategies and engaged in coaching sessions with us have successfully shifted their leadership practice to intentionally build relationships, create collective capacity, and distribute leadership that accelerates movement toward a shared vision. By deepening their self-awareness, these leaders were able to empower their teams and lighten their loads as they embraced a more collaborative approach to leadership.

Go Do

No matter how many educational theories we understand or how much advice we take on as leaders, experimenting and implementing new behaviors on the job is the only thing that will change our practice. Here are some ideas to help you become a leader who is able to make meaning:

1. Try crafting your vision using a combination of the rubber band and Me Us It models. Even better, invite your team to co-create a vision using these tools.
2. Find an opportunity to intentionally use See Hear Speak to really build rapport and trust. Make a conscious effort to see first, hear second, and speak last. Reflect on your experience afterward.
3. Identify someone with whom you don't agree. Take 15 minutes to reflect and practice stepping into their shoes using the Presence Triangle. Aim to really understand their perspective and commit to taking one action based on your new insights.

4. Apply the D × V × F > R formula to a change you are trying to make. Do you have all three elements? If not, plan how you will identify and strengthen the missing element so your change can be successful.

Don't feel the need to take on all these ideas simultaneously. Select one that feels relevant now; you can always revisit these challenges later.

Reflection Questions

- What are your key insights from this chapter?
- How can you use the MESSY tools to ensure your leadership supports meaning making in your school?
- Which go-do activity will you experiment with?
- What did you learn from these actions?

3

E for Emotional Connection

Key Challenge: How can I build trust?

Uncommon Sense: Addressing conflict can lead to great trust and, therefore, deeper relationships.

John, an elementary school principal, was proud of his ability to build relationships with his staff, striking a healthy balance between being professional yet still very personable and relatable. However, things started to shift, and John felt the changing dynamics within his team. He began to doubt the integrity of his leadership team and no longer felt he could trust them as he previously had. Sensitive conversations among the leadership team were shared much more broadly, breaking a sense of confidentiality, and John was worried about how to address his concerns without damaging the relationships he had worked so hard to build.

For a while, he avoided tackling any underlying issues since he knew it would require him to have a series of challenging conversations. It wasn't until John talked through possible scenarios with his coach that he found the courage to be honest. He recognized that avoiding difficult conversations wasn't just derailing the leadership team's collective work; it was eroding individual relationships among those on his team. John was losing the deep emotional connections he prized because of the unspoken "elephants in the room." Once he mustered the courage to be honest and start to address the underlying issues, he was pleasantly surprised at how many members of the team reacted positively.

John had feared it would feel awkward and he would end up feeling isolated. To be fair, he did indeed have to invest considerable time in multiple conversations with two of his less confident, more defensive colleagues—listening to their concerns, rebuilding trust, and reassuring them that he would support them as they addressed the issues together—but others responded well and stepped up to face the discomfort. Some even looked relieved that the issues were finally being addressed. John realized he wasn't alone; the entire team saw signs that things weren't working well and was actively avoiding having tough conversations and sharing honest feedback.

Once the proverbial door had been opened, John took the opportunity to organize group learning about how best to approach hard topics and provide one another with feedback. The team developed common language and utilized feedback frameworks to help them navigate complex topics—both now and for the future. As a result, John not only felt more confident but also developed a stronger connection to his team. Engaging in the difficult conversations together had built deeper trust and understanding.

> *"Having the courage to be honest—I can't believe what a difference it made!"*

Developing stronger emotional connections is a shift from a mindset of "I am focused on my relationships with my team and stakeholders" to a mindset of "I have the courage to build deeper and more honest relationships within my school and community."

Most school leaders are all too aware of the importance of relationships. However, they may not be fully aware of the tension that exists for leaders to be professional, build personal connections, and create a collaborative culture. Whereas in the past, you could simply put on a professional persona at work, nowadays people expect to be able to talk about a range of personal, sensitive, and even controversial issues—and they expect leaders to be real.

We have coached hundreds of principals and department heads in situations similar to John's. Many leaders strive for a "culture of nice" at any cost—patching over tensions, avoiding feedback, and ignoring underperformance. By doing so, they may superficially succeed in keeping everyone happy, but they lose the opportunity to build more honest, deeper relationships. Unintentionally, they also end up creating relationships in which many things are left unsaid and problems are pushed below the surface. One of our coaches framed this issue neatly: "For the most part, school leaders lead in really nice environments—maybe too nice. As a result, any confrontation is pushed underground and likely has been for so long that it makes it that much harder to surface, and it requires more courage of the leader to tackle problems that have been ongoing for years."

Of course, it isn't just relationships with teacher colleagues that matter in schools. The very nature of schools requires leaders to be caring and emotionally connected to *all* their stakeholders, not only teachers and staff but also students, parents, and key community members. Leading in a so-called culture of nice may be easier in the short term, but over time, the niceness of the culture may very well be the roadblock to improvement or forward progress. The uncommon sense of relationships is that addressing conflict can ultimately lead to a stronger level of trust and therefore a deeper relationship.

Times of uncertainty can create a need for stronger, more honest relationships. Sometimes, very personal conversations need to be a part of the work.

Indeed, this was once frowned upon in the workplace, but leaders now find great value in their ability and willingness to listen even when it is uncomfortable and to engage in challenging conversations they cannot control. Courage to build deep and meaningful relationships requires connection, trust, and honest feedback.

How MESSY Are You?

Before diving further into emotional connection, take a few minutes to reflect on your own leadership. How would you rate yourself on the different aspects of the Emotional Connection MESSY Monitor (Figure 3.1)? Where might a close colleague or friend rate you? Do you take the time to build meaningful and honest relationships with your team, or are your relationships more surface-level and transactional? Your self-reflections are a great place to begin, but to accelerate your leadership development, invite someone on your team to weigh in and share

FIGURE 3.1
Emotional Connection MESSY Monitor

Emotional Connection Behaviors	Never	Rarely	Sometimes	Frequently	Very Often
I have deep, trusting relationships with colleagues.					
I know how to use powerful questions to get to the heart of an issue.					
I deliver consistent, effective feedback to those around me.					
I regularly ask for feedback on myself.					
I create an environment where all staff feel safe contributing, being themselves, and challenging one another.					
I am confident engaging in difficult conversations when necessary.					
I can create a positive relationship dynamic even within a difficult conversation.					

their insights. After all, this chapter is about encouraging more feedback! (An aggregate rubric, which combines each chapter's MESSY leadership monitor, can be found in Appendix A.)

If you found yourself selecting *Frequently* or *Very Often*, then these are likely areas of strength for you. However, if you found yourself selecting *Never* or *Rarely* on some of the items, then these are probably areas of struggle for you. The strategies and tools (Iceberg Model of Relationship, Feedback Traps, WWW-EBI, A FIRM Framework) shared in this chapter are designed to support you in building your leadership capabilities to have a stronger emotional connection.

Laying the Foundation

Regardless of the type of school or district, we consistently hear from school leaders about the importance of connection and trust. Sometimes, we hear this from veteran principals who sense that many of their working relationships are too surface-level and leave too much left unsaid. Other times, we hear from leaders moving into new roles or new schools who need to invest in building relationships with new colleagues. Occasionally, we coach teachers as they are promoted or transitioning to a leadership role and need to reconfigure their relationships with colleagues whom they suddenly find themselves managing. Finally, we also support superintendents and other district-level leaders who oversee dozens of schools and need to build trusting relationships with principals they may only see face-to-face every few weeks.

In all these cases, building trust in relationships requires deliberate effort. Viviane Robinson (2017) identifies building relational trust as one of three critical leadership capabilities for effective school leadership. Trust is a fundamental building block of all relationships and requires reliability, acceptance, openness, and congruence. You build a partnership or relationship with someone when you feel close to and trust them. As relationships develop, they naturally go through different stages. With that in mind, the iceberg model of relationships allows us to view and understand three different dimensions of relationships.

> *"Moving from a 'culture of nice' to a 'culture of trust' really resonates for me. Nice will not suffice!"*

Social

The social dimension is often where a relationship begins—the tip of the iceberg. It serves primarily as a way to get to know individuals by asking them about their general interests (e.g., their families, favorite sports, favorite TV shows, weekend plans). As leaders, it's important to get to know the people with whom we partner so our relationships don't feel transactional or impersonal. The social dimension is important, but if the relationship never progresses to the other realms, then it will only ever be superficial at best.

Business

The business dimension—analogous to the bit of the iceberg visible above the water but beneath the tip—is where good work gets done. This is where two people develop and demonstrate a strong level of respect and understanding for each other's values and roles. This foundation helps people accomplish a variety of tasks or goals. In most organizations, leaders invest heavily in the business dimension of relationships, as seen in processes, meetings, and organizational structure. If the business dimension is smaller than the social one, it may be hard to make tough calls or objective decisions.

Trust

The trust dimension—the submerged base of the iceberg that can be deep underwater—is where we feel comfortable expressing vulnerability and concerns. This dimension includes all four cornerstones of trust:

- Reliability: You keep the commitments you've made and help others follow through on their commitments.
- Acceptance: You accept others through your actions and behaviors, not just your words.

- Openness: You are open with your thoughts and feelings toward others; few secrets and surprises exist between individuals.
- Congruence: You engage in honest communication, as evidenced by a connection between your inner experience and your outward expressions; this is built on personal integrity and straight talk.

This is where the relevance of the iceberg analogy comes into play. The three dimensions are not three equal layers; the sheer volume of "underwater potential" is incredibly deep but not easily visible. Although building deeper emotional connections takes work, every relationship has potential once you take the time (and the courage) to go deeper, beneath the surface.

John found the iceberg model to be a real eye-opener. He realized the "good old days" he was missing from earlier in his career were actually founded on surface-level relationships. Although he was a natural at fostering the social dimension (e.g., taking an interest in colleagues' families and personal interests, putting them at ease) and he had successfully fostered the business dimension of his working relationships, he hadn't managed to deepen those relationships to the trust dimension. Consequently, neither John nor his colleagues felt able to voice their vulnerabilities or concerns. They didn't stray into difficult emotional territory, they didn't address the unspoken elephants in the room, and they didn't have the courage to engage in difficult feedback conversations. It was only once John took the bold step of modeling the way—by becoming more open himself and by broaching more challenging conversations—that he was able to experience the richness of more trusting, deeper relationships.

Building Trust

If your relationships tend to fall into one of the first two dimensions (i.e., the top two layers of the iceberg), there are various strategies you can use to build trust and move into the third dimension. The first strategy is to make sure people truly feel seen and heard by you. In Chapter 2, we shared a simple but effective tool (See Hear Speak) that, when used consistently, works to build trust. Taking the time to see and hear another person makes them feel valued and helps you connect at a deeper level.

> *"I will slow myself down to build trust first, before expecting that all our teachers will respond to my requests of them."*

You may have already had some training in reflection or listening skills . . . or maybe this isn't a natural strength of yours. One technique that can really help you to hear others better is Playback. This is one of the most fundamental, yet underused, listening tools. If we want people to feel heard, the best way to convey that is to simply "play back" what they said, using their own words when possible. This is especially effective because it forces us to listen to the other person's voice instead of our own. Summarize and paraphrase what they've said, using phrases such as "So, what you're saying is . . ." or "Let me make sure I got this right . . ." You can also incorporate their feelings and your intuition:

- "What did you feel when that happened?"
- "He/she said . . . ?"
- "It sounds like you've got some concerns about . . ."
- "Can you say more about . . . ?"
- "I imagine that was very frustrating/upsetting."

Another simple strategy to build trust is self-disclosure. This can happen at several levels and help humanize a leader. The simplest level of disclosure includes sharing one's thoughts, a deeper level involves sharing one's feelings, and the deepest level includes sharing one's needs and values. The deeper the level, the greater the trust. Think about how you can (constructively) disclose feelings, needs, or values with members on your team to build more trust. Over time, skillful and authentic self-disclosure can lead to greater feelings of trust in the workplace.

John incorporated self-disclosure with his leadership team when working to repair collective trust. He shared how the breach of confidentiality affected him and caused him to question leveraging the collective wisdom of the group to instead rely on his own instincts and experience. As John became more comfortable sharing his thoughts, concerns, and worries, he noticed the level of connection growing within the team. Others began to share their thoughts and feelings more openly, and the conversations felt much more honest as a result.

Self-disclosure neatly links with the notion of vulnerability. Many school leaders are already familiar with Brené Brown's famous TED talk (2010) and subsequent book on the power of vulnerability (2013). Brown's research vividly illustrates how those who are prepared to be vulnerable naturally build strong relationships with others. In her work, she uses the word *wholehearted* to describe people who can live from a place of vulnerability.

Giving Feedback

One of the most powerful ways to build deeper emotional connection and trust with others is through feedback. Inviting feedback from another person makes you vulnerable and shows very powerfully that you are interested in their perspective and are committed to self-improvement. Likewise, giving thoughtful and constructive feedback to another person shows that you are committed to their development and trust that your relationship is strong enough to broach sensitive issues.

Nevertheless, most school leaders we coach are deeply uncomfortable with feedback—so much so that *feedback and difficult conversations* was the top development need that arose from our analysis of coaching conversations. Perhaps this is unsurprising, given that feedback strikes at the tension between two human needs: the need to learn and grow and the need to be accepted just the way you are. As a result, both giving and receiving feedback requires understanding and the management of a lot of feelings (Heen & Stone, 2014).

Everyone needs feedback to perform at their best because feedback gives us information about how we are doing against expectations. It's only with feedback that we can calibrate our performance and improve practice. The strange paradox is that although leaders may be uncomfortable *providing* feedback, most people thrive when they *receive* it. Unfortunately, in many schools, there is a lack of substantive feedback and a general acceptance of "this is the way we've always done things." In some cases, performance issues have been allowed to continue for years, making it more challenging for those leaders who do strive to improve practice by providing effective feedback.

Many leaders assume that people don't like receiving feedback, yet recent data challenges this perspective (Officevibe, 2022):

- A majority 65 percent of staff report they would welcome more feedback.
- Some 40 percent of staff report being "actively disengaged" when they receive little or no feedback.
- There is a 15 percent lower turnover rate in organizations that implement regular feedback.

Shifting a Culture Using Feedback

Ava, an experienced teacher and department head, was working hard to shift the culture within her English department. The school had a history of students getting strong scores in English, but some staff members had settled into complacency as a result. Ava could see that a few individuals weren't performing at a level she expected of all her teachers. Even though Ava could identify specific gaps in performance, she was anxious and uncomfortable providing feedback because she hadn't had positive experiences in the past. She felt that feedback conversations usually escalated into win-lose scenarios without ever having the desired impact. As a result, Ava was hesitant to have feedback conversations because she didn't want to damage relationships. She knew feedback conversations were a critical part of the improvement process, but she actively avoided them at all costs.

She explained to her coach how much she valued her working relationships: "I have worked at the school for almost 14 years in a range of roles and consider many of the staff my friends. I feel unsettled if I hear staff are disgruntled, and I take it as a personal mission to find a solution so everyone is happy. I feel the same about all stakeholders. I want to be liked, and I want to know that everyone feels happy."

Ava talked openly in coaching sessions about her struggles with feedback, and her coach was able to help her recognize that she wasn't focusing on giving *balanced* feedback. She was only ever considering negative feedback without providing any positive feedback. As Ava reflected on her own experiences, she shared how uncomfortable receiving positive feedback made her feel. Personally, she had a hard time accepting positive feedback because she could only see all the work ahead that still needed to be done. Without realizing it, her own self-talk about positive feedback was getting in the way of her ability to share positive feedback with others.

Ava assumed that what worked for her would also work for members on her team—a one-size-fits-all method of feedback. Identifying this blind spot helped

Ava see the benefits of reframing feedback conversations. She no longer viewed feedback conversations as "all or nothing" conversations that would escalate and potentially create awkward moments. Indeed, Ava's entire approach to feedback changed. "I realized that some challenging conversations may not be challenging in that the person may not even know there is an issue. I want to remember to go into every conversation with curiosity and wonder rather than judgment." Through practice and utilization of feedback frameworks, Ava learned how to balance conversations so feedback included both highlighting things that were working well and identifying areas for improvement.

Ava isn't alone in her discomfort with feedback. Many school leaders fall into the trap of either avoiding feedback altogether or providing only negative feedback as a means of improvement. As leaders look to help others improve, it can be easy to forget the need to balance out the conversations, recognizing that feedback can and should highlight the positive aspects of an employee's performance. Research shows that the single biggest factor differentiating high-performing and low-performing teams is the ratio of positive to negative feedback. Within high-performing teams, there are six pieces of positive feedback given for every piece of negative feedback. By contrast, there is only one piece of positive feedback given for every three pieces of negative feedback in low-performing teams (Zenger & Folkman, 2013). The message is clear: People need and crave positive feedback to perform at their best.

Rather than labeling feedback as either positive or negative, it may be helpful to use the terms *on-track feedback* and *off-track feedback*. This naming shift can help reframe the notion that feedback isn't about good versus bad or right versus wrong. Instead, it's about how someone's performance is helping or hindering them from reaching a mutually desirable goal. Giving on-track (positive) feedback establishes a safe environment for the off-track (negative or constructive) feedback. Ultimately, the presence of frequent feedback creates a feedback culture where people are unafraid to have feedback conversations, which in turn become a normal part of the workday. An easy rule of thumb is that more feedback is generally better, and organizations with a strong feedback culture typically outperform on metrics such as employee engagement and tenure. A Gallup poll of 65,000 employees found that those who received strengths-based feedback tended to be better performers and had turnover rates that were nearly 15 percent lower than those of employees who received no feedback (Asplund & Blacksmith, 2011).

Identifying and Overcoming Obstacles to Feedback

Intellectually, most school leaders agree that feedback is essential for improvement, yet there remains a general hesitancy to give feedback. Ask yourself, "Why do I shy away from giving feedback?" Whatever your reason, know that you aren't alone! Our coaches are kept busy every week helping school leaders shift their mindsets and practices around feedback. In fact, this is one of our most common coaching requests. In the words of one coach, "Sometimes leaders avoid difficult conversations because they are worried about upsetting people. They may feel that their school culture is dependent on goodwill and close relationships. They don't want to risk these relationships; they want to be liked and not hurt the feelings of others."

> *"I avoid crucial accountability conversations; I avoid giving feedback on poor behavior and missed commitments. I say, "No worries," but that's not what I'm feeling."*

Figure 3.2 shows the five most common feedback traps that prevent leaders from giving feedback, together with a shortcut workaround to help you overcome each barrier. Take a moment to reflect on which of the feedback traps you tend to fall into. (Don't despair if you can relate to many of them!) Consider the workaround(s) suggested. Will they work for you? What other ideas do you have

FIGURE 3.2
Feedback Traps

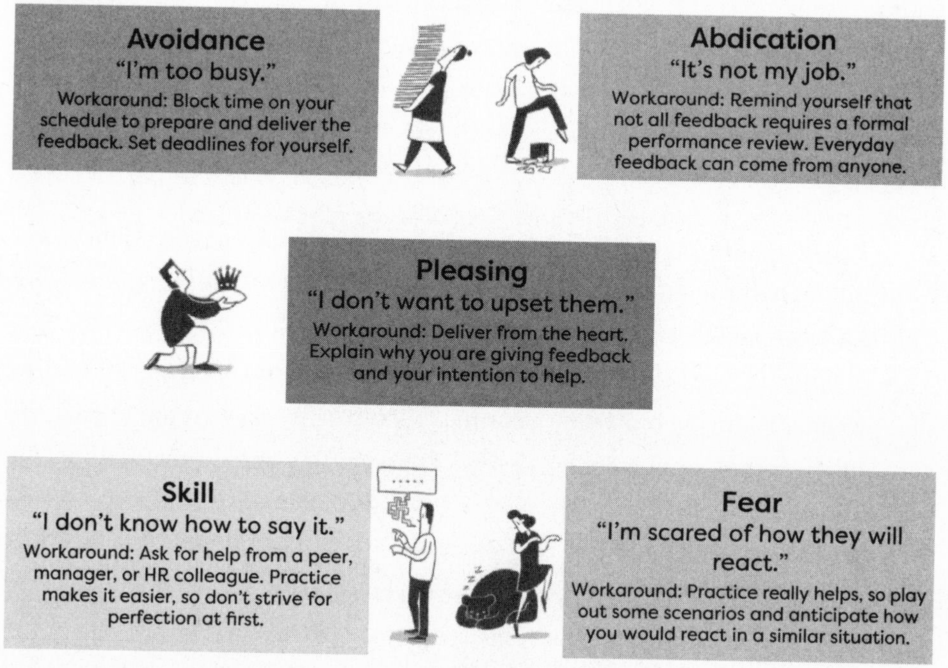
Avoidance
"I'm too busy."
Workaround: Block time on your schedule to prepare and deliver the feedback. Set deadlines for yourself.
Abdication
"It's not my job."
Workaround: Remind yourself that not all feedback requires a formal performance review. Everyday feedback can come from anyone.
Pleasing
"I don't want to upset them."
Workaround: Deliver from the heart. Explain why you are giving feedback and your intention to help.
Skill
"I don't know how to say it."
Workaround: Ask for help from a peer, manager, or HR colleague. Practice makes it easier, so don't strive for perfection at first.
Fear
"I'm scared of how they will react."
Workaround: Practice really helps, so play out some scenarios and anticipate how you would react in a similar situation.

to help you avoid these feedback traps? If you want to create a culture of feedback, consider sharing these traps with colleagues and have an open and honest conversation about feedback.

John reflected on the common feedback traps with his coach and quickly discovered that he was falling into the avoidance and pleasing traps. He had always taken pride in his ability to work well, both personally and professionally, with colleagues, so he didn't want to do anything that risked upsetting those relationships. He always assumed that feedback would be hard to give and difficult to receive.

The human brain is both amazing and a little strange. We're all hardwired to react to perceived threats, so what do you think happens to most people when they hear, "Can I give you some feedback?" This perceived threat puts people into fight, flight, or freeze mode. You've likely experienced this yourself. What was your reaction the last time someone asked you that question?

The good news is that as a leader, you can take steps to minimize a negative response and help people see feedback as the gift it is. To help your team ensure that your feedback is received in the spirit it is intended, try the following strategies:

- Provide more regular feedback by making feedback conversations a frequent, helpful, and normal part of the workday. This means giving feedback not just when something exceptional happens.
- Practice using *I* statements (e.g., "I feel upset when I see you responding to emails during our team meetings"). This helps explain the impact the other person's behavior has on you personally, which they may not be aware of.
- Be conscious of your body language and tone of voice. Wait until you are in an emotionally balanced state to provide feedback.
- Pick a neutral setting. Sometimes the boss's office may not be the most inviting place for an open discussion. The unbalanced power dynamic could create a perceived threat that triggers a fight, flight, or freeze reaction. It's important that the other person is in an emotionally balanced state to receive the feedback.
- Remind yourself that feedback is about creating a dialogue toward a mutually agreed outcome.

When Ava first considered the feedback traps with her coach, she was a bit shocked. It was like looking in a mirror! She had been a department head for many years and knew she had a reputation for success, yet she also knew deep down that over the years she had continually shied away from giving feedback and avoided addressing patterns of poor behavior by a few colleagues. When she started talking with her coach, Ava saw that she would rationalize this to herself in terms of not wanting to upset the other person and aiming to keep everyone happy—the pleasing trap. She had had some bad experiences with negative feedback in the past, so she was fearful of how the other person would react and was worried that giving them feedback could make a bad situation worse—the fear trap. She also assumed that all feedback conversations were all-or-nothing conversations that required her to raise big performance issues, and she felt poorly equipped to do this—the skill trap. Ultimately, she never got around to broaching the issues at all—the avoidance trap.

Ava's coach asked her to reflect on what the impact was of her continually avoiding giving any feedback. Ava realized that the most dedicated teachers in her department were being influenced by a small number of colleagues whose lack of commitment and poor behavior were going unchecked—whether they were skipping rostered duties, not keeping noise levels reasonable in their classrooms, or missing assessment reporting deadlines. It was demoralizing for the rest of the staff who sometimes had to step in for their less committed colleagues so students didn't suffer.

Ava knew she needed to start giving her colleagues more feedback and normalize a feedback culture on her team. She started by increasing her own comfort with feedback by including a feedback culture on her team. Much of this was positive, on-track feedback, since many of her colleagues were dedicated, hardworking, and performing well. She then resolved to bite the bullet with a couple of the complacent teachers who weren't pulling their weight. With the help of her coach, she planned and rehearsed an important (and long overdue) feedback conversation with one of them. She made sure to frame the feedback as factual observations, not vague judgments, and was clear about her requests for the teacher moving forward. In the end, she was pleasantly surprised. She managed to stay calm and balanced the need to listen with the need to be clear around expectations. The teacher was prickly at first but started to acknowledge that some of his behaviors fell short of expectations. Ultmately, he agreed to Ava's requests.

Buoyed by this success, Ava started to feel a lot more confident about giving feedback. She was determined to not allow situations to escalate in the future but instead use feedback much more regularly to guide colleagues' off-track (and on-track) behaviors.

Using Feedback Frameworks

Here are two frameworks you can use to structure your feedback conversations. The WWW-EBI framework shown in Figure 3.3 is a much-loved, memorable feedback tool you can weave into your conversations to give more regular, everyday feedback. It ensures that you balance on-track and off-track feedback and can underpin your deliberate move toward a feedback culture in your school. It consists of the question "What went well?" and the prompt "Even better if . . ." That's it!

FIGURE 3.3
WWW-EBI Framework

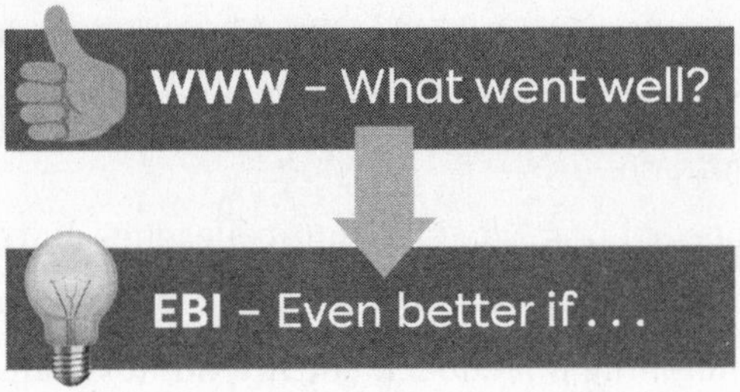

This framework is especially easy to model. Do you want feedback at the end of staff meetings? Ask colleagues to share something that worked well and an idea that would make it even better (or they can jot down ideas on sticky notes as an exit ticket). There are many opportunities to model asking for feedback, and regular use of WWW-EBI can help normalize feedback and familiarize everyone with some language around feedback.

We have heard many different stories from school leaders who have gone on to integrate WWW-EBI into the fabric of their school life. Principals have used the framework to guide midyear performance appraisal conversations, instructional coaches have used it to give teachers feedback after lesson observations, and teachers have used it to solicit feedback from students at the end of a lesson. The WWW-EBI framework is great to give and receive everyday feedback about general topics. No matter how time-poor you are, you can easily incorporate it into your daily practice and use it in brief conversations and interactions.

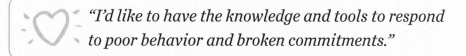

> *"I'd like to have the knowledge and tools to respond to poor behavior and broken commitments."*

However, what about when you need to address a more major pattern of behavior that is negatively affecting the school culture or student learning? How can you effectively prepare for a more complex difficult conversation? In this case, WWW-EBI clearly isn't the right tool; it doesn't provide an opportunity to go into enough depth to really challenge and shift an ongoing problem. Instead, try the A FIRM framework (Figure 3.4) to structure these feedback conversations. It takes a little more planning—requiring you to think through the **a**genda, the **f**acts, the **i**mpact, a **r**equest, and **m**utuality—but the results are well worth it.

FIGURE 3.4
A FIRM Framework

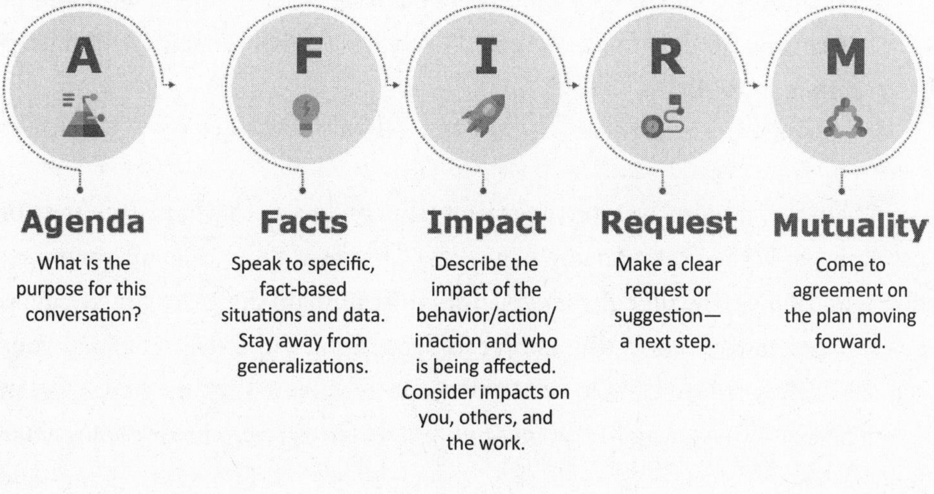
A
F
I
R
M
Agenda
What is the purpose for this conversation?
Facts
Speak to specific, fact-based situations and data. Stay away from generalizations.
Impact
Describe the impact of the behavior/action/inaction and who is being affected. Consider impacts on you, others, and the work.
Request
Make a clear request or suggestion—a next step.
Mutuality
Come to agreement on the plan moving forward.

Let's work through an example of how you might use the A FIRM framework. Suppose you need some assessment data from a colleague to complete a report. You haven't received the data despite a few gentle nudges. This isn't the first time you've had this problem with this particular colleague, and you'd like to address it with them. Here is how you might plan your conversation:

- **Agenda:** "Hi. I'd love to have a conversation with you about how we work together to get student reports out on time. Is now a good time to talk?"
- **Facts:** "For the latest round of student reports, I received the assessment data from you two weeks after the deadline, and I gave you two reminders. Last year, the situation was similar."
- **Impact:** "I couldn't start writing my report until I had the assessment data from you. This meant that I only had one week left to write 180 reports. I had to work right through the weekend. I missed out on watching my son's final match of the season, had to give apologies to my friend for missing her birthday celebration, and left my partner caring for our three kids all weekend. I'm worried that the reports I wrote aren't the best, since I had to rush them."
- **Request:** "Next time, I'd like us to sit down in advance and agree on a deadline for your assessment data to be ready. Then I'd like you to commit to getting the data to me on time. That way, I can block out my time and do a good job with the reports."
- **Mutuality:** "What do you think? How could this work better?"

Of course, this isn't a monologue in practice! You will need to do plenty of listening while the other person is speaking. However, there is an art to finding the right balance. During the conversation, you can share the facts (which should be clear and indisputable), the impact (on you, others, and the work) and your request. This sets the scene for you to then have an open conversation with the other person—the mutuality stage—to come to an agreement regarding your request. The A FIRM framework can be used to help guide almost any potentially difficult conversation. The key to using the framework successfully is preparation. Make sure you are very clear on the facts and impacts in advance.

> *"I have applied the A FIRM model in a number of situations, and it makes difficult conversations easier. It keeps them on track and helps people see the impact of their actions."*

Inviting Feedback Can Build Emotional Connections

So far, we have explored how you can confidently give feedback to team members, but to create a feedback culture, school leaders need to get comfortable giving feedback and learn how to receive and actively solicit feedback. John Hattie emphasizes the dual importance of giving and receiving feedback in his "ten mindframes" for educators, one of which is simply "I give feedback and act on feedback given to me" (Hattie & Zieler, 2017). Inviting feedback may feel awkward at first, but you will be amazed at how your openness to receiving others' feedback can build trust and deeper emotional connections with them.

Once you ask for feedback, it's crucial to know how to respond graciously to that feedback. You don't want to end up blindsided or instinctively want to challenge a comment that feels unfair. Most people receiving feedback tend to go through (or get stuck on one of) three stages:

1. **Denial:** It's not always easy to accept feedback. Try to assume good intentions and acknowledge what you are experiencing. A simple "thank you" might be all that is needed.
2. **Exploration:** Try to see the feedback from the other person's perspective. Even if you don't agree with it, see if you can find the 2 percent of truth within it. It may help you identify blind spots.
3. **Integration:** Choose your response to the feedback and think about how you want to integrate the feedback into your learning.

Keep in mind that all feedback is a gift, and your response to that gift can be as simple as a "thank you." That may be all you need to say in the moment. If it's the right time, you can choose to have a conversation, but if you aren't in the right place emotionally, a wise choice may be to simply thank them for the feedback and share that you may want to talk further at another time.

Moving From a Culture of Nice to a Culture of Trust

In this chapter, we explored what it takes to build deep emotional connections. MESSY leaders realize that a so-called culture of nice—of keeping everyone happy and not rocking the boat—has its limitations. To build deeper, more trusting relationships, you need to go beneath the surface of the iceberg and intentionally create a feedback culture in which both giving and receiving feedback is a way of life. Doing this will call on you to be open, honest, and vulnerable.

> *"I realized that it doesn't have to be a tradeoff between high expectations and strong relationships. You can be kind on the person but tough on the issue."*

Our coaches see, time and time again, the difference that this shift can make on school leaders' personal effectiveness and leadership practice. One coach summed this up: "It's helpful when leaders can shift their mindset about having difficult conversations, so they can see that being honest and providing honest feedback is being fair to the other person. It's not about upsetting someone. It's about honestly providing information to help them improve."

Go Do

No matter how many educational theories we understand or how much advice we take on as leaders, experimenting and implementing new behaviors on the job is the only thing that will change our practice. Here are some ideas to help you become a leader who is able to forge strong emotional connections:

1. Use playback and disclosure strategies to deepen trust with a colleague.
2. Model asking for feedback using the WWW-EBI framework.
3. Prior to your next feedback conversation, use the A FIRM framework to plan what you're going to say.

Don't feel the need to take on all these ideas simultaneously. Select one that feels relevant now; you can always revisit these challenges later.

Reflection Questions

- What are your key insights from this chapter?
- How can you use the MESSY tools to ensure your leadership builds emotional connection in your school?
- Which go-do activity will you experiment with?
- What did you learn from these actions?

4

S for Sensing the Future

Key Challenge: How can we adapt fast enough?

Uncommon Sense: Long-term plans can become straitjackets, whereas fast-cycle experiments enable you to respond to changing needs.

Nicola, a BTS Spark coach, was coaching a group of literacy teachers who were helping struggling students boost their literacy skills. Their state department of education had introduced new literacy support teacher roles in every secondary school to support targeted students, and the intention was clear. Students struggle to flourish in their upper years of schooling without having attained a baseline level of literacy. However, the role of these new literacy teachers was not well defined. Individual schools were left to flesh out how the positions would work. Without job clarity, there was huge potential for the support teachers to step on other teachers' toes.

It wasn't clear if the literacy support teachers should pull out students for individualized tutoring or work alongside them in their regular classes. Some support teachers found themselves barred from entering the students' classes since some subject-area teachers felt threatened by having another adult in the classroom. In addition, department heads weren't clear how the support teachers complemented their schoolwide work. In the first year of implementation, many of these new teachers appeared like deer in the headlights. They were stunned, confused, and without any clear direction for how to approach their role. They were waiting for someone to clear up the confusion and give them instructions. Similarly, many school principals found themselves waiting for clarity from the district or state level—where leaders were reluctant to mandate the implementation details and expected schools to decide how to use the new positions in ways that best met the needs of their students.

Throughout the first year, a few of the literacy support teachers started to embrace the lack of clarity and took the opportunity to explore what was possible. They stopped waiting for permission and started experimenting with different ways of working—for example, pulling out small groups of students for intensive support rather than individual students and collaborating with teachers in different subject areas.

As a coach, Nicola stimulated their thinking by asking questions such as "What's your vision for this new role? Where are you stuck? What's holding you back? What might you experiment with?"

For Mark, this was an a-ha moment: "I remember suddenly realizing in the middle of one of my coaching sessions that this was a once-in-a-career opportunity to do what I felt was most needed, to respond to the needs of my students. I had release time to work with them and nobody was telling me what I had to do. It wasn't a poisoned chalice; it was a gift." Mark seized the opportunity, invested time in building bridges with key colleagues in his school, and trialed a range of innovative approaches (including utilizing a zero period, creating interest groups, and implementing peer tutoring to support his students). He made some early breakthroughs with notoriously hard-to-reach students, word spread, and interest in his literacy support strategies increased among his colleagues.

Mark was an early pioneer of the literacy support teacher role; he embraced the uncertainty and lack of clarity, had the personal agency to make sense of the role in his school context, and was courageous enough to trial new approaches in collaboration with colleagues. He had a vision, could sense the future, and was willing to experiment and take risks—but the feeling of discomfort (felt by many of his colleagues) with being given free license to make sense of a new policy initiative is a natural one.

We have learned that many school leaders are accustomed to strict, rules-based environments where policy guidance often dictates what should be accomplished and how. In many cases, educational organizations, whether it be school districts or individual schools, suffer from institutional inertia and a cultural resistance to change. Education systems, which are often complicated and under continual public scrutiny, can be slow to adapt to change. On top of these cultural constraints, many school leaders are exhausted, time-poor, and managing all the "should-dos" involved with running a school. Taking the time to dream big, creatively investigate, and imagine a different type of future for their school feels like a luxury many school leaders just can't afford.

Nevertheless, this is exactly what our schools need. We need agile and adaptive learning communities with leaders who can slow down enough to see the big picture, challenge the status quo, and experiment with new solutions to create the future they want. These are leaders who can sense the future, which is a significant shift from a mindset of "I create strategic plans for the future of our school but feel limited by constraints" to one of "I am energized by possibilities and run fast-cycle experiments to contribute to an ever-evolving plan for the future."

Most of us are wired to make sense of the future with reference to the past. *Sensing the future*, though, requires a different orientation to planning. Typically, schools utilize a comprehensive school improvement planning process that involves all stakeholders; covers a three- to five-year period; and outlines the school's vision, mission, and strategies to achieve stated goals. There may be aspects of continuous improvement planning embedded in the strategic plans that consider things like yearly growth, new needs, and opportunities, but strategic plans are primarily static documents. That doesn't mean they're inherently bad, but when the future has so many unknowns, holding tightly to static strategic plans may limit growth and contribute to stagnation. Unintentionally, these plans can become straitjackets.

In our research, we've found that the most successful leaders are those who don't feel bound by their strategic plans. They are leaders who can envision multiple possible futures and run fast-cycle experiments. They spend time imagining ways their school can evolve, and they lead with this in mind—constantly adjusting their approach as new information emerges. Admittedly, sensing the future requires a shift in leadership that may not be easy. As one of our coaches shared, "Most school leaders I coach want to focus on the future, but they get sucked into managing the immediate needs and never quite get out of the day-to-day to plan for a different future."

If that feels familiar, know that sensing the future is a mindset and skillset that can be learned. With that in mind, this chapter is filled with strategies and tools to help you slow down, think outside the box, and imagine new approaches to tackle current challenges—all skills of leaders who can sense the future.

How MESSY Are You?

Before diving further into sensing the future, take a few minutes to reflect on your own leadership. Are you guilty of getting caught up in the processes of planning, or do you feel free to experiment with bold new ideas? Do you have a wish list of improvements to be made, or have you settled into feeling like things are good enough? Take a moment to rate yourself on the Sensing the Future MESSY Monitor (Figure 4.1). Consider asking a colleague or friend to rate you, too. (An aggregate rubric, which combines each chapter's MESSY leadership monitor, can be found in Appendix A.)

FIGURE 4.1
Sensing the Future MESSY Monitor

Sensing the Future Behaviors	Never	Rarely	Sometimes	Frequently	Very Often
I slow down enough to see the big picture.					
I constantly strive for improvement in a way that creates real impact.					
I am curious and invest time in understanding more, often seeking out how others might view the same issue.					
I have the courage to act on ideas and create experiments to try out new approaches.					
I persevere with experiments, continually reviewing and seeking the right solution.					
I can find simple solutions to complex problems.					
I nurture a culture of curiosity and experimentation with my team.					

If you found yourself selecting *Frequently* or *Very Often,* then these are likely areas of strength for you. However, if you found yourself selecting *Never* or *Rarely* on some of the items, then these are probably areas of struggle for you. The strategies and tools (Rivers of Thinking, Breakthrough Thinking Cycle, Asking Three Whys, Bop It) shared in this chapter are designed to support you in building your leadership capabilities to better sense the future.

Slowing Down and Reconnecting to Your *Why*

One of the top needs we uncovered from our coaching work with school leaders is the need to slow down. Our coaches hear stories from leaders who are so busy implementing policies and putting out fires that they don't have time to think!

The act of slowing down should be intentional and reflective. This isn't about self-care, although most leaders would really benefit from prioritizing their own self-care more. Rather, this is about learning to press the pause button. It's a shift from putting out fires to taking the time to discover the source of the fire—or, even better, figuring out how to prevent the fire from starting in the first place. One principal captured this well, sharing, "I want to give myself the permission and headspace to step back in my own mind and be more balanced in the way I operate and lead." Another leader shared, "My brain is going 1,000 miles an hour. I need to slow down."

> *"I need to move into a wiser, more reflective style of leadership, like Mr. Miyagi in* The Karate Kid.*"*

Slowing down should become a time of purposeful and intentional reflection. Unfortunately, there is no magic solution for this. It starts with giving yourself permission to pause and is built into a habit with intentional practice over time. (If you are struggling to imagine how you could ever find the time to create a new habit, Chapter 5 includes some tools and ideas to help with prioritization and time management.) With so much to accomplish, it can feel counterintuitive to pause, but strategic and creative thinking are more likely to occur when we switch off. New ideas arise when we allow ourselves time to reflect, think, and wonder. They don't occur when we are stressed or exhausted.

To cultivate a pause and reflect habit, try scheduling time in your calendar. Perhaps it's 10 minutes in the middle of the day with your office door closed or maybe you carve out 15 minutes before your commute home to reflect on the day's accomplishments. It doesn't matter when or where. Your goal is to create consistent space in your schedule for you to pause, think, and reflect.

Does the Future Need Managers or Leaders?

Giving yourself permission to pause also offers the opportunity to become more mindful about your leadership. Think for a minute about your day-to-day activities. Would you characterize most of your actions as *leading* or *managing* your school? There may be some overlap, but, simply put, management is about the present and leadership is about the future. Management focuses on the implementation of current practices, making sure they are successful and efficient. Managers can improve current systems, but they don't drastically change the direction of a school or the way things are done. The problem with only managing is that it may never lead your team to new and improved approaches, and in some cases, it can have you focusing on things that aren't even important. As Peter Drucker (2006) once said, "There is surely nothing quite so useless as doing with great efficiency what should not be done at all" (p. 83).

By contrast, leadership is all about sensing and charting a new future. Successful leaders have a future destination in view and a willingness to take a bold approach to reach that destination. The reality is that schools need both managers and leaders. Schools must have capable managers of the present, but they also need leaders who are dissatisfied with the way things are and challenge the way things are done. As a school leader, it's easy to overfocus on management and underfocus on leadership because managing relies on existing paradigms, whereas leadership requires us to break out of our patterns of thinking.

> *"Sometimes I feel as though I need to rescue people from the demands of the job. This leads to little time for reflective and big-picture thinking, planning, and implementation. I now recognize that if I spent time thinking and planning, I might improve their job."*

Rivers of Thinking

It is human nature for our brains to form thought patterns—neural pathways or so-called rivers of thinking—to get through our daily activities. To better understand this concept, developed by Edward de Bono (1993), create a mental image of water running down a mountain. It may start as a series of slow drips or scattered streams, but the water eventually comes together and flows in the same direction, creating deep grooves or pathways over time—even cutting through rock and creating gullies. These pathways are a good analogy to what happens with our thinking. We develop deep mental pathways that influence how we interpret information, what we see in the world around us, and how we respond. It's not all bad. These rivers of thinking help us extract order, make quick decisions, and create expertise. These patterns are why we can go through our morning routine without much thought or drive to work without directions. They help us survive and are essential to how we work and live.

However, our rivers of thinking can also trap us with ingrained ways of thinking, causing us to spend time defending old patterns that block creativity. As a result, we end up with a biased approach in our thinking and ignore the many possibilities available to us. So, even though rivers of thinking can help us manage our day-to-day life and work, they don't help us innovatively solve problems or develop new ways of working. If we always stay with our same old patterns of thinking, it's almost guaranteed that we'll get the same old results. The good news is that you can break free from your rivers of thinking, challenge the way things are done, be open to new approaches, and create new mental pathways—all of which is very much needed to sense the future.

Breakthrough Thinking Versus Average Thinking

Unfortunately, too many school improvement projects fade without a trace. Those that have a lasting impact succeed because they're championed by teams of teachers and leaders who truly embrace the notion of continuous improvement not as buzz words but as an actual practice. They are always looking to learn and improve, and they use constant dissatisfaction to fuel their work. Although some leaders naturally engage in continuous learning and improvement, having a framework (e.g., design thinking, action learning, breakthrough thinking cycle) makes it so much easier to lead a team through the process. There are slight differences in each framework's approach, but all are iterative in nature and focus on continuous improvement.

The school leaders we coach have had great success using the breakthrough thinking cycle to lead their teams to think differently. Breakthrough thinking is distinctly different from average thinking as it involves a constant pursuit of what might be possible. As you read through the two different types of thinking (see Figure 4.2), notice where you or your team naturally struggle.

These leadership attributes in Figure 4.2 are the key behaviors that underpin the five steps of the breakthrough thinking cycle (Figure 4.3). You'll notice that each step requires your attention to be focused in a different way—you need to look in a different direction. The cycle offers a systematic way to tackle entrenched school improvement issues. First, the problem is defined, then time is taken to collect data and reflect on what is currently happening. This data and the observations are analyzed, and potential causes are identified. An idea is developed to address these causes, and a plan is finally put together to implement it. If the problem isn't fully solved, then the cycle repeats.

You'll obviously have natural strengths and weaknesses in the way you think your way around this cycle. This means you'll likely get stuck, underplay, or skip over parts of the cycle. There are common traps leaders and school teams fall into when using the breakthrough thinking cycle. In the following sections, we share the essence of each attribute, identify a mental trap that can hold people back, and offer a strategy that can be used on a school improvement issue.

Challenging the Status Quo: *Looking Up*

Imagine you're an activist. Activists are dissatisfied with the present, tend to challenge what currently exists, and want to build a better future. Activists are constantly striving for improvement in a way that creates real impact. Activists don't accept current assumptions and actively seek out opportunities for improvement. In short, activists challenge the status quo.

Challenging the status quo, however, is often undermined by the so-called reasonableness trap. Most problems are not new, and surely, it's assumed, current

FIGURE 4.2
Breakthrough Thinking Versus Average Thinking

Leadership Attribute	Breakthrough Thinking	Average Thinking
Challenging the Status Quo	• Constantly strives for improvement in a way that creates real impact. • Not happy with current assumptions and actively tries to find new ways of looking at the future of school.	• Thinks they are doing a good job. • Works hard and assumes their efforts are "good enough." • Accepts things the way they are. • Views current attempts to improve performance as "the best we can do."
Inquiring	• Looks at every angle for potential improvement • Looks for opportunities to experiment and try new angles. • Is curious and invests time in understanding more, often seeking out how others might view the same issue.	• Has strong opinions about one or two things that could get better. • Is under pressure from tasks, cannot make time for new learning and exploration.
Analyzing	• Gets to the root cause of a problem and understands it from a systemic point of view. • Takes time to really think things through.	• Tries or dismisses ideas without analyzing their full impact. • Often retries new solutions to the same problem.
Solving	• Finds simple solutions to complex problems. • Sees a path to action that will move things forward. • Creates experiments to test and learn.	• Tends to spend too much time seeking the "right" solution rather than moving into action. • Holds back from actioning or making change.
Persevering	• Perseveres with an issue and experiments, continually reviewing and seeking the right solution. • Doesn't give up when things don't work the first time around.	• Abandons ideas and solutions. • Becomes disheartened after an attempt to improve something after one or two failures.

FIGURE 4.3
Breakthrough Thinking Cycle

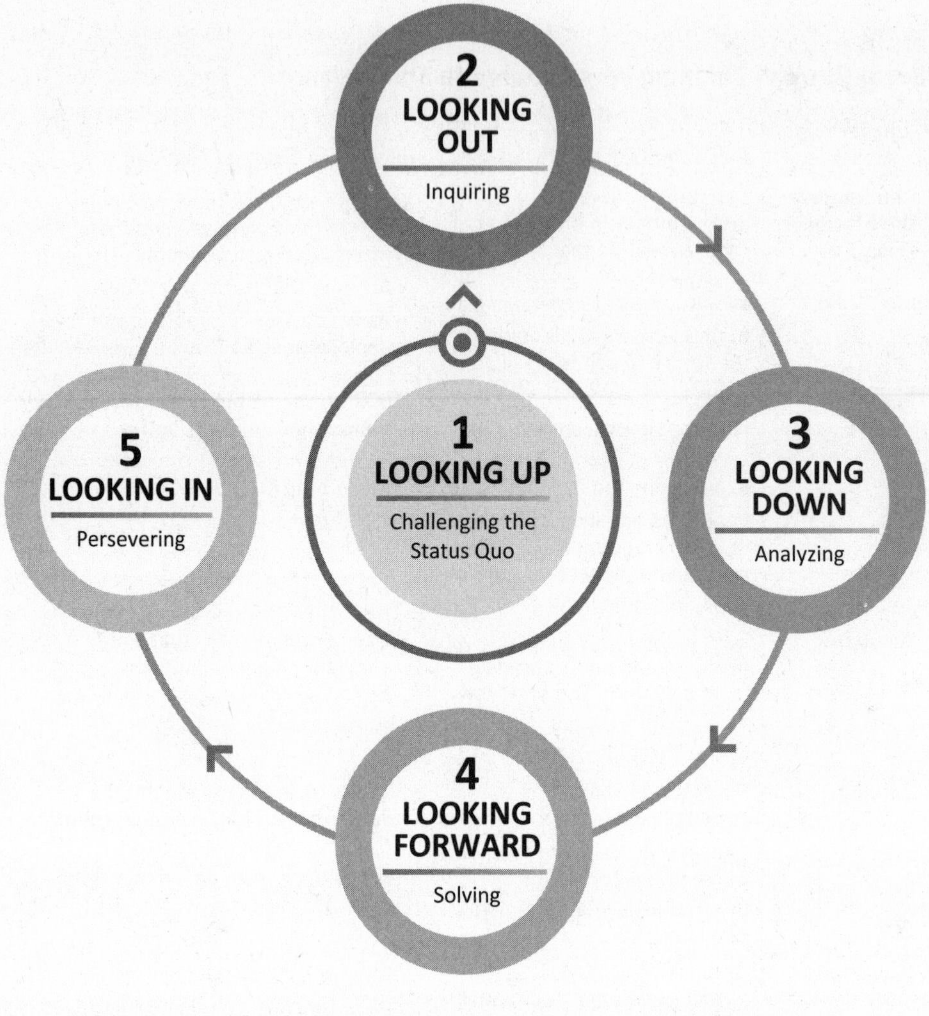

practice is there for a reason. Things *must* have been tried before to change the current state, which has no doubt persisted because it's the best possible solution or situation. In the end, the "reasonable" explanations become limiting beliefs and keep people from trying new solutions.

Let's start working through an example. Jennifer, an elementary school principal, was always looking for ways to improve her school and noticed that parents weren't attending back-to-school nights or parent-teacher conferences. It would have been easy for Jennifer to get caught up in the reasonableness trap and think, "Parents just don't value education" or "There is a lot we *could* do, but my teachers are just too overcommitted right now." Instead, Jennifer raised the problem with her team as a challenge to solve collectively. Leaders who are great at sensing the future don't accept "reasonable" explanations; they are always looking to surface and bust these beliefs. So where to start?

There's no point spending time and energy challenging the wrong problem. Therefore, before you can begin solving the problem, you must first understand the *right* problem. The goal is to identify a problem that is realistic but challenging, purpose-driven, and exciting. If you aren't sure where to look, try keeping a bug list. As you are working, keep a running list of things that, well, bug you. Hidden within this bug list will be all sorts of problems to be solved (Kelley & Kelley, 2013). Once you've identified a suitable problem, you can then frame it using these three questions:

- What is the problem we are trying to solve?
- Who is it important to and why?
- How can we turn the problem into an inquiry question?

Reframing your issue as an inquiry question such as "How might we . . . ?" or "What can we do to . . . ?" can be extremely helpful. In Jennifer's case, the problem to be solved was low attendance at parent-teacher conferences. It is an important problem to solve because it prevents parents from being a full participant in their child's education. Jennifer's team tried to frame the problem in a few different ways: "How might we redesign parent teacher conferences to increase attendance and participation?" "How might we engage with our parents in new and different ways to support students' learning?" The phrase *How might we . . . ?* invokes a collaborative and inclusive approach that fosters teamwork and collective problem-solving. It implies that everyone is a part of the solution and invites participation from all stakeholders.

> *"I found that framing our school improvement issues as inquiry questions has opened up dialogue and participation from many more staff. There is a sense of optimism, creativity, and 'can-do.'"*

Inquiring: *Looking Out*

For this step, imagine you're a researcher—always curious, inquiring, and thirsty to know more. Researchers are willing to investigate every angle for potential improvement—even when that means looking outside their industry or field for inspiration and ideas. This step of the breakthrough thinking cycle is all about being curious and investing time in understanding more. It also means staying on top of current trends not only in schools but also in other sectors and thinking about the applicability to the future of schools.

In our experience, this part of the cycle is often the weakest and undermined by the pragmatist trap. School leaders are busy, and many think they have a pretty good idea of what is going on in their school. Spending time being inquisitive and asking vague open-ended questions seems like a luxury they can't afford, so they leapfrog straight to solutions based on the data with which they are already familiar. It would have been all too easy for Jennifer and her team to assume that parents were simply not interested in their children's education, but what if that weren't the case? What if parents had time but didn't find the parent-teacher conferences valuable or felt intimidated and uncomfortable in school settings? Great leaders avoid jumping into potential solutions without first gathering new data. They know the benefit of curiosity and actively spend time seeking to understand more. Once an issue is identified, leaders can step back to see the big picture, which helps them notice both frustrations and assumptions.

The best way to reveal frustrations and get to the root of a problem is to talk with the individuals most affected. Although the process is often time intensive, leaders can learn a lot by talking to parents, teachers, and students—depending on the problem to be solved. The goal here is to let go of your own assumptions and find out what people are experiencing. Taking time to identify and understand frustrations can help you more fully understand the problem. A few useful phrases to gather new data include *What is your experience with . . . ? Tell me more about . . .* and *What are your views on . . . ?*

Jennifer and her team questioned their assumptions about how they engaged with parents (e.g., conferences should always be held in person, in the evening, and for a predesignated amount of time) and surfaced frustrations from both parents (e.g., "It's an effort to attend, and I get so little time with the teacher") and teachers (e.g., "The parents I really want to talk to rarely attend"). Once the team talked with parents, they learned that some parents struggled to get to school and had to weigh the challenges of their weekly evening routine against whether it was worth the 10-minute conversation. Even those parents who did attend didn't find the conferences to be particularly helpful. In short, the team revealed that almost all parents failed to see much value in the conversations. Almost immediately, Jennifer's team began to see the problem from different perspectives.

Analyzing: *Looking Down*

Now imagine you're a detective, analyzing the situation and trying to get to the root cause of the problem. The analyzing step is about taking all the data you've collected and looking through it—analyzing it—to uncover potential factors that directly lead to the problem.

At this point, you may be wondering, when are we actually going to get to *solving* the problem? Stay with us because you're not alone. The analyzing step is frequently undermined by the solution trap: becoming seduced by the search for a solution too soon. Eager to solve the problem, it's easy to jump from data to solution. For example, leaders discover something (e.g., parents find the teacher-parent conferences intimidating) and immediately try to implement a solution (e.g., make conferences more inviting by adding refreshments). However, when they do this, they bypass true analysis and risk not actually solving the problem.

Great leaders help others suspend their tendency to jump to a solution too hastily. When we spend more time thinking, we often come up with a better answer. As Albert Einstein is often quoted as sharing, "If I had an hour to solve a problem, I'd spend 55 minutes thinking about the problem and five minutes thinking about the solution."

A simple strategy you can use to analyze your data involves digging below the surface and asking three *whys*. This helps you uncover the root cause of the issue you are tackling. Take one of the factors that is contributing to the problem and ask *why* this is happening. Then take the answer to that question and again ask *why*. Repeat a third time using the answer to the second question.

Question #1: "Why are parents not engaged in the school?"
Answer: "Because they don't feel part of it."

Question #2: "Why don't they feel part of it?"
Answer: "Because they find it intimidating."

Question #3: "Why do they find it intimidating?"
Answer: "Because there is a culture gap between teachers and parents, we don't do much to bridge that gap, and we do not make school welcoming and accessible to parents."

In this case, the school identified the root cause to their problem of low attendance at parent-teacher conferences: They are not welcoming or accessible to parents. Let us be clear—identifying and recognizing the root cause is essential. It helps you create more relevant, innovative, and effective solutions.

Solving: *Looking Forward*

For the fourth step, imagine you're an inventor, proposing new solutions and creating prototypes or experiments that iterate those solutions. This step of the cycle is all about brainstorming, playing with new ideas and then turning them into fast-cycle experiments. Some teams get stuck in this step when perfectionism kicks in and they fall into the perfectionist trap. Most people are naturally reluctant to share ideas if they aren't fully formed because they don't want to appear foolish, so they stay quiet—or, once ideas are on the table, they let the failings and inadequacies of their preferred solution dominate the conversation. In either case, they hold back from having the courage to try something different and bring new ideas to life. Sensing the future requires leaders to be bold and think big, but it also requires leaders not to take themselves so seriously. Adding levity and fun to the process can help your team avoid the perfectionist trap.

One strategy that can help overcome this trap is to play with the rules that bind your current challenge. These could be actual requirements or just organizational norms people have accepted as rules (which is often the case in schools).

Once you've identified the rules, it's relatively easy to identify which ones can and should be challenged. To do this, we use the basic idea behind the electronic handheld game Bop It that was popular back in the 90s. Anyone remember playing this game? It was designed to test your reflexes and coordination by giving you commands to "bop" a button, "twist" a dial, or "pull" a lever. Consider the rules that govern how things are currently done . . . and *bop 'em*!

Jennifer's team identified the following rules for parent-teacher conferences that her school accepted as normal:

- Parent-teacher conferences are scheduled, in-person events held at school.
- Conferences take place in the evening, effectively forming an additional duty for teachers (and working parents) after a normal working day.
- Every parent is invited and has a set amount of time with the teacher.
- A student's report card provides the basis for the conversation and is created at the end of every quarter.

Now let's bop it! Figure 4.4 shows how Jennifer's team reshaped the rules of parent-teacher conferences and rethought the entire process.

For this kind of brainstorming to work well, your team needs to be sufficiently open to change, willing to think big, and able to embrace their creativity. They also need to be sufficiently comfortable thinking and operating outside of the proverbial box. This might require some groundwork from you ahead of time.

As you begin to share ideas, don't worry if some of them sound unrealistic. The future of education needs your big ideas. Big ideas can always be scaled back, but small thinking has nowhere to go. The next time you're feeling nervous about sharing a big new idea, remember that someone in a meeting once took a shot and said, "Let's make a movie about a tornado full of sharks." Out loud. And that person wasn't laughed out of the room! Not only that, but to date, there have been an astonishing six *Sharknado* films.

We aren't necessarily suggesting that you should create outlandish ideas, but give yourself permission to play, dream, and even be wrong. You can ground your thinking by asking, "What would have to be true?" for each of your ideas. Don't discuss or argue about what is currently true; it's enough to just acknowledge it.

FIGURE 4.4
Using "Bop It" to Rethink the Rules

Prompts	Reshaped Answers
Stretch it, shrink it . . . • How might you stretch the rule to infinity? • How might you shrink the rule to nothing? What if it didn't exist?	• Parents are invited to meet with teachers weekly. • Parent-teacher conferences don't exist. Parents engage with teachers via an online dashboard, and Facetime or Zoom meetings are set up as needed.
Twist it, turn it . . . • How might you reshape, reuse, repurpose, or shift the rule?	• Every parent is invited, but different parents have different needs and might need different times or ways to connect.
Whack it, smack it . . . • Whack your problem 100 years into the future. What rules would still apply? • Smack your problem 100 years into the past. What rules would your predecessors have followed?	• Not sure if any of the rules will apply in 100 years. • A century ago, conversations were limited to mail correspondence and one-way conversations—from school to home.
Spend it, save it . . . • What would the problem look like with infinite resources? • What would the problem look like with no additional resources?	• With infinite resources, we could create interactive digital portfolios that showcase student work and could be viewed by parents. We could compensate teachers to conduct home visits. • With no additional resources, we could leverage the technology we have for better accessibility.

With ideas on the table, you can start to convert them into possible solutions for the future.

Persevering: *Looking In*

For this final step, imagine you're an ant, diligently working your way around obstacles, carrying a load, and never being diverted from the bigger purpose. The last step of the breakthrough thinking cycle is, of course, implementation. We have deliberately labeled this behavior as persevering because true breakthrough thinking rarely works the first time. Effective breakthrough thinkers need to be able to stay resilient and creative as they iterate their way to making their solution land. They're constantly testing, experimenting, and learning, so they're constantly refining their breakthrough thinking.

Fast-cycle experimentation is a process of quickly testing and validating ideas or proposed solutions through a series of iterative experiments. This is where you turn insight into action by testing ideas. You don't have to implement every idea or implement ideas across an entire school; rather, you can test things out with one class, grade level, or project. Create a prototype and learn from implementation. Ask questions such as *What can we learn from this?* or *How can we overcome this?* You may need to remind others of your original intent with a phrase such as *Let's not lose sight of what we are aiming for*.

> *"I need to have the same approach that I encourage my students to have—be courageous. I can do it. I can try new things. If it doesn't work, I can scrunch it up, throw it away, and try something else."*

Jennifer and her team learned so much as they worked through the breakthrough thinking cycle. They learned that parent-teacher conferences weren't accessible to all parents, and they brainstormed a variety of potential solutions (e.g., virtual parent-teacher conferences, student-led conferences, Saturday conferences, interactive digital portfolios, online feedback forms). Not all their ideas will work, but Jennifer's team began testing them out in small experiments with specific grades. Implementing ideas such as these on a small scale can create opportunities to learn and share with the broader staff. Importantly, the experience can be shared, and the team can learn from the fast-cycle experiment by reflecting, "What worked well? What were the challenges? How can we overcome them? What have we learned that will inform our future work?"

Admittedly, architecting a plan is no easy task, but this is often not where people fall short. People tend to give up too easily while implementing the plan. If the goal is too lofty and your ambitions are too high, then it's likely you will (either partially or wholly) fail. When an idea fails, your instinct may be to change direction, water down your ambition, or give up completely. This is known as the achievement trap. The trick is to rise above these instincts and be confident in the learning *process*. If you focus on learning and growth, it will be easier to maintain high expectations through continuous experimentation until you see success.

Practicing breakthrough thinking with others can help create a culture of learning and nimbleness that is key to sensing the future. The more you practice, the more flexible your thinking will become and the better you and your team will get at thinking through problems and trialing innovative solutions. To support your work, we have included a helpful breakthrough thinking guide in Appendix B. Keep in mind that not all solutions will work, at least not in their first iterations, but they will provide valuable insights and keep you moving forward. Once you have evidence that a solution isn't working in its current form, you may need to course correct, iterate, or back up a step or two in the process.

A principal once shared with us how using the breakthrough thinking cycle helped create a bigger change: "Our staff is in the middle of a culture change. I see us collectively moving from a mindset of 'things are already tough here, so we don't need any added pressure' to a mindset of 'things are tricky everywhere and we all need to help each other improve the future.'"

A leader who can sense the future is a leader who knows how to pause, takes time to think, and guides their team through iterative cycles of problem-solving. This allows them to create a nimble strategic plan, positioning their school at the forefront of education. Indeed, leaders who can sense the future are invaluable to schools since they can help ensure that their school remains relevant and responsive to the evolving needs of students and society.

Throughout this chapter, we presented some strategies you can use with colleagues to expand their thinking. Of course, helping others make a mental shift to confidently sense the future is more complex than making the shift yourself. Therefore, you may also need to draw on strategies in other chapters, such as See Hear Speak and the Presence Triangle in Chapter 2 (to build trust and understand fears and concerns) or the ETC coaching process in Chapter 6 (to overcome mindtraps that are holding staff back from innovating).

Good luck with your efforts!

> *"Leading a high-performing school means that we can all too easily stay on a familiar path and avoid taking risks. I'm planning to initiate a bugs list with my team to prevent us from being complacent and help us embed a culture of continuous improvement."*

Go Do

No matter how many educational theories we understand or how much advice we take on as leaders, experimenting and implementing new behaviors on the job is the only thing that will change our practice. Here are some ideas to help you become a leader who is able to sense the future:

1. Identify how a river of thinking may have affected your ability to work through a problem recently. Commit to how you will do one thing differently next week to deliberately break out of this river of thinking.
2. Identify two areas where you want to challenge the status quo and frame each problem into an inquiry question.
3. Share your inquiry questions with your leadership team or staff and select one to solve utilizing the breakthrough thinking cycle.

Reflection Questions

- Which of the five breakthrough thinking attributes would you like to strengthen in your own practice? Why?
- What are your key insights from this chapter?
- There were many MESSY tools introduced in this chapter. Which would most help you sense the future—slowing down enough to see the big picture, challenging the way things are done, or trying new approaches?
- Which go-do activity will you experiment with?

5

S for Seizing Momentum

Key Challenge: How can I take control of how I spend my time?

Uncommon Sense: You have more freedom to choose how you spend your time than you ever imagined.

Stephen was an administrator responsible for leading an amalgamation of schools in his region. It was a complex project with multiple stakeholders and lots of moving pieces. Over a period of months and after a series of consultation meetings, he began to win the support of both school staff and parent communities. Stephen started to feel more confident in his leadership of the amalgamation; it was a big change, but he knew it would better support students. He started to generate excitement about the future reorganization, but then there was a surprising about-turn decision by the department of education. Despite all the work completed and progress accomplished, his superiors abruptly canceled the amalgamation—citing budgetary constraints. Somewhat shocked, Stephen had to resist becoming critical of the head office and their directives. After all, their actions left him feeling triggered and even a bit deceived and betrayed. Perhaps timing was on his side, though, since the decision was made just before a holiday break, giving Stephen a much-needed opportunity to step away—so he could return with a new perspective and mindset.

Instead of feeling stuck and frustrated by all the directives and policies that came down from the state department of education, he realized he could make changes from where he led, despite top-down directives. He had a responsibility to ensure that decisions and policies were enacted, but he was still trusted to prioritize his time and could decide where he devoted his attention, the nature of the relationships he built with his schools, and how he introduced new initiatives. This was a lightbulb moment for Stephen. He took control of his schedule. He dedicated time to working with his network of principals to co-create a vision for improving education. He was meticulous about how he spent his time—aligning his effort and actions toward supporting schools as they strove to achieve their collective vision. He became comfortable shedding or delegating less important tasks.

Yes, Stephen was still beholden to the policies and directives coming from the department of education, but he learned to be selective with how he implemented those policies. He started viewing all directives and policies through the lens of the bigger vision, and he then introduced and implemented them with principals by prioritizing the aspects that were aligned with their collective school improvement vision.

Stephen's leadership inspired staff in schools throughout the town. Principals were motivated and generated a culture of collective efficacy in their teams. Student attainment data started to show an upward trend, and Stephen was invited to present his approach to fellow directors across the state. As Stephen shared, "I am finding ways to have conversations about what we can do and capitalize on every small win. It's becoming contagious as everyone is now talking about the difference *we* can make."

It would have been easy for Stephen to feel (justifiably) outraged by the policy U-turn and adopt a victim mindset, yet he had the self-control to choose a different path. You may not be a superintendent or in a district administrative role, but you undoubtedly find yourself needing to respond to new policies and changes. How do you react to change? Do you find yourself sliding into a victim mindset, or do you have the personal agency to seize momentum?

Sometimes things happen in education that we don't expect—or don't even like—but we always get to choose how we respond. Stephen may not have anticipated such an abrupt course correction, but he chose to seize momentum by acting on what was in his sphere of influence and reframing how he would handle policies and directives moving forward. Seizing momentum is a shift from a mindset of "I focus on process and attempt to manage a high-quality education for students" to one of "I am clear on the difference we want to make and focus on activities that yield better outcomes."

In our coaching work with education leaders, we've seen countless examples of leaders who realize they are "doing their best on autopilot." In other words, they get through each day by responding to situations and fulfilling regular commitments in their schedules while not feeling in control or able to prioritize what matters most. Sometimes leaders develop an overreliance on process and existing practices, which can be comfortable but can also derail them from getting things accomplished. Working with a coach, these leaders learn to become more proactive and deliberately make choices rather than staying in a reactive mode. As one coach shared, "Many school leaders I coach have a constant sense of not getting enough traction on what's important. What helps is revisiting their values (i.e., what's important) to get off the treadmill. Then they can get creative about getting some things done quickly using the 80/20 rule, realizing that a small number of activities can have a disproportionate impact on outcomes."

Schools are busy places with lots of complicated moving pieces and constant distractions. Without a concerted effort, it's all too common for leaders to get sucked into the daily grind and lose sight of the work they really want to push forward with. Seizing momentum is about staying focused on that big audacious goal your team has set and learning how to flex on some of the other leadership tasks to make progress on the work that matters most. It is about being an action-oriented leader.

How MESSY Are You?

Before diving further into seizing momentum, take a few minutes to reflect on your own leadership. Where would you rate yourself on the Seizing Momentum MESSY Monitor (Figure 5.1)? Where might a close colleague or friend rate you? Are you a proactive leader making deliberate decisions to move your team forward, or do you find yourself stuck in a reactive leadership mode? (An aggregate rubric, which combines each chapter's MESSY leadership monitor, can be found in Appendix A.)

FIGURE 5.1
Seizing Momentum MESSY Monitor

Seizing Momentum Behaviors	Never	Rarely	Sometimes	Frequently	Very Often
I am purposeful and know the kind of impact I want to have.					
I understand that attention is the key to getting things done.					
I feel in control of my time and how I choose to spend it.					
I prioritize the most important tasks first, rather than just the "quick wins."					
I understand why I procrastinate and know how to avoid it.					
I stay focused on the bigger goal, despite setbacks, and I never give up.					
I can focus on outcomes—not the process.					

This MESSY monitor is a great self-reflection tool, but it could also be valuable for you to share with your team. Does your leadership team have clarity on the work that matters most? Do they know how to prioritize work? Creating space for this conversation may not only give insight into where your team members are but also give them permission to recalibrate their to-do lists. If you found yourself selecting *Frequently* or *Very Often*, then these are likely areas of strength for you. However, if you found yourself selecting *Never* or *Rarely* on some of the items, then these are probably areas of struggle for you. The strategies and tools (Three *P*s, Eisenhower Prioritization Matrix, Push and Pull of Change) shared in this chapter are designed to support you in building your leadership capabilities to better seize momentum.

Focusing on the Work That Matters Most

The concept of seizing momentum is not a new one. Stephen Covey centered some of its core tenets in his hugely popular *The 7 Habits of Highly Effective People* (2013). He named the first habit *be proactive* and the third habit *put first things first*. The essence of the latter is the idea that effective people prioritize their activities based on what is most important, rather than on what is most urgent or easiest to do. They focus on activities that align with their values, mission, and long-term goals, and they manage their time effectively to ensure they are spending it on activities that are truly important.

Be proactive means taking responsibility for your own life and not allowing external circumstances to dictate your actions or reactions. This can be a particular challenge if you are leading a school in a struggling socioeconomic community, where the odds that both your students and your educator team are facing can feel overwhelming. Nevertheless, there are many examples of schools and students overcoming huge disadvantages. According to Covey, people have the power to choose their response to any situation and proactive individuals take the initiative to create positive change and pursue their goals—rather than wait for someone else to solve their problems or dictate the direction they should take.

Together, these two habits emphasize the importance of taking control of your own life and work and of focusing on what is truly important—and taking action to make progress toward your goals. Both habits are at the heart of seizing momentum. This chapter will show you how to be an action-oriented leader, seize momentum, and get things done by focusing on the three *P*s: *proactivity, procrastination,* and *prioritization.* As you read, reflect on which of the three *P*s are supporting or hindering your personal effectiveness right now.

Proactivity: Exploring Drive and Focus

Being proactive in a leadership role requires both drive and focus. Most school leaders tend to have incredible drive—it's what helped them reach their leadership positions—but drive can be hard to sustain over the long haul, especially when work gets tough. Channeling drive is key to an action orientation stance of leadership. After the reorg setback, Stephen had to dig deep to stay motivated and compelled to continue improving educational outcomes for students, but his drive led to a townwide collective vision of school improvement.

Daniel Pink, author of *Drive: The Surprising Truth About What Motivates Us* (2011), defines *drive* as a motivational state that occurs when three fundamental psychological needs are satisfied: autonomy, mastery, and purpose. Autonomy refers to the desire to direct our own lives and make our own decisions. Mastery refers to the urge to get better at something that matters to us. Purpose refers to the yearning to do what we do in the service of something larger than ourselves. According to Pink, these three needs are essential for achieving and maintaining a state of motivation and engagement in any task or activity.

Angela Duckworth (2016) has another take on drive, which she has popularized with the concept of *grit* as a key hallmark of high achievers. Rather than being exceptionally talented, Duckworth argues that these people succeed due to a combination of passion and perseverance. She studied a variety of groups, including teachers working in some of the toughest schools and students in the National Spelling Bee. In her research, she found that grit results from the ability to both sustain interest in and demonstrate tremendous effort toward very long-term goals. In short, individuals who are gritty tend to be more self-controlled.

What drives and motivates each person is unique, but we can harness our individual drive to improve our ability to be an action-oriented leader. There are four characteristics of drive that contribute to action orientation. As you read through these characteristics, take note of areas where you are already strong and other areas you may want to develop:

1. **Aspiration:** a hunger for success
   - ✓ Possesses a desire to work hard to achieve goals.
   - ✓ Is purposeful and personalizes the kind of impact they want to have.
   - ✓ Has a competitive edge.
   - ✓ Works to understand, meet, and exceed standards of excellence.
2. **Self-Assurance:** belief in oneself
   - ✓ Has confidence in their own ability and purpose.
   - ✓ Is rarely oversensitive and shows few doubts about their talent.
   - ✓ Demonstrates resilience and durability.
   - ✓ Has confidence when tested and confronted with obstacles or negativity, such as hostility, unwillingness to cooperate, or failure.
   - ✓ Holds a longer-term vision while working toward current goals.
3. **Initiative:** ownership
   - ✓ Is quick to take responsibility and slow to blame others.
   - ✓ Is forthright and willing to challenge in a constructive, outspoken way.
   - ✓ Takes on challenges they enjoy along with ones that are less exciting.
   - ✓ Is prepared to test themselves in new and uncomfortable ways.
4. **Focus:** attention on the critical
   - ✓ Understands that attention is the key to getting things done.
   - ✓ Prioritizes the most important tasks first, rather than just the quick wins.
   - ✓ Is organized and systematic in their approach.
   - ✓ Stays engaged until the work is done.

If you decide to consciously work to increase your action orientation, drive, and focus, you may be surprised at how big an impact you can have. As you seize momentum and harness your own sense of personal agency, you can serve as a role model for others. Driven by a shared vision and a strong sense of collective efficacy, you and your team can be a powerful force.

Procrastination: The Problem with Putting it Off

Considering the pace at which our world moves, having drive and taking initiative aren't always enough. Taking an action orientation to the next level requires us to dig deep and overcome the feelings that hold us back from experimenting or trying something new. Whether it's just discomfort or distaste for a specific task—or something deeper, such as fear, anxiety, or insecurity—adjusting your behavior requires you to identify the feelings, beliefs, and values behind the procrastination to get to the root cause of the issue.

Procrastination is nothing new. It's a good bet that it is something you have experienced both in your personal and in your professional life. What might surprise you, though, is the realization that procrastination is not a time management problem but an emotional regulation issue that can be overcome by acknowledging feelings and shifting mindsets. It's important for leaders to take a proactive action-oriented stance, but it's equally important for leaders to explore what is happening when they struggle to get motivated or find themselves procrastinating. Contrary to popular belief, procrastinating does not mean doing absolutely nothing. When people procrastinate, they can still be exceptionally busy—but they tend to be busy with less important work. Being busy allows them to avoid engaging with the more important work to be done. School leaders may also find themselves procrastinating because they are exhausted; they can't find the energy to focus on what they know is important, so they keep themselves busy with other, less critical tasks. (Chapter 6 provides some pointers to help with self-management.)

Leslie, the principal of a large urban school, found herself procrastinating to avoid implementing one of the two key goals she set for herself for the school year: getting into classrooms to stay connected with student learning. With a large

teacher team and more than 1,000 students, it was easy to become distant from what was happening in the classrooms.

Leslie shared with her coach, "I get stuck in my office. I want to be more present with teachers and students. How do I balance that without having to take work home?"

Leslie's coach probed a bit, "How difficult is it to visit classes? What strategies have you tried?" Together, they uncovered that there were two mindset issues getting in the way of Leslie spending time in classrooms. First, she felt guilty about taking advantage of the relative luxury to visit classes when her to-do list was piling up on her desk. Second, when Leslie walked into classes, she was aware that her appearance as principal might be an interruption, which made her feel uncomfortable.

She shared that she wasn't entirely sure what she should do on the visits. The discomfort Leslie felt during the visits kept her from prioritizing this work on her calendar. It was just easier to let her calendar fill up with other work. Leslie's coach gently helped her challenge the idea that class visits were a luxury; when she took time to reflect, Leslie could see that they were a vital part of her role in improving teaching and learning. Together with her coach, she created a checklist for her class visits. She listed what she wanted to observe, identified students she might want to check in with, and determined how she would follow up. She even created simple conversation starters, so she was ready for a conversation when she walked through the classroom doors.

With these simple self-created tools, Leslie started blocking time on her calendar for class visits. She did this with intention, thinking through the best time of day for each class to be visited and enlisted the support of her administrative assistant to help protect that time on her calendar. Leslie kept a small notebook and would quickly jot down notes for herself after each visit. She noted what she observed, any follow-up requirements, and—most important—how she felt about the visits. Leslie's feelings were very important, because it was the initial feeling of discomfort that led to her procrastination. Having effectively shifted her mindset around class visits, Leslie no longer procrastinated and was able to prioritize the work she felt was important.

Of course, the benefits weren't just felt by Leslie. Her teachers started feeling more valued. Even though they were at first a little uncomfortable with being observed, they soon realized that Leslie's intentions were good. They enjoyed having a professional conversation about their teaching, reflecting on their professional practice, getting another perspective, and gaining new strategies. The feeling soon spread. Some teachers opened up and became eager to talk with colleagues about pedagogy in the staff room. Gradually, the quality of teaching throughout the school started to improve, and there was more consistency from class to class. The ultimate winners were the students.

Is there a task you have been actively avoiding at work? If so, try to consider the emotions attached to that task. What are you feeling? What is your self-talk? What might be the root cause of your procrastination? Once you gain clarity about what you are avoiding and why you are procrastinating, you can start to address them just like Leslie did with the classroom visits.

Here are a few tactics to move past procrastination:

- **Reward yourself:** Come up with a creative way to reward yourself for changing your behaviors.
- **Forgive yourself:** Every time you find yourself falling into a procrastination trap, stop, forgive yourself, and move on.
- **Eliminate the catalyst:** Remove anything that tempts you to fall for the procrastination habits—for example, social media apps, using email instead of in-person conversations, answering emails instead of diving in and doing more important work.
- **Have compassion for yourself:** Imagine you were talking to someone else with the exact same problem. Speak to yourself as if you were showing compassion and empathy for that person, helping them to see the "why" behind the issue.
- **Reframe the task:** Once in a good space, find a way to reframe the task to have a positive spin.
- **Break it up:** Divide what feels like an enormous task into smaller pieces. Focus on achieving one piece at a time.

Prioritization: The Trick of Decluttering

Now that you've worked through critical mindset shifts around action orientation and procrastination, it is time to focus on building the tactical day-to-day toolkit that will help you get things done. In this section, we'll think about how we spend our time and what systems we can put into place to help us prioritize and act on items effectively. School leaders commonly share that they need help with prioritizing. The key, thankfully, is simple. The first step is to create structure and systems that help us make conscious choices about our time.

> *"I want to be able to prioritize the things that are most important, but it's not easy as I get easily sidetracked."*

Peter DeWitt (2021) has been a strong advocate for educators to reprioritize their activities:

> What we do need to do is look at whether we are engaging in compliance activities because we have policies in our heads that make us believe we are supposed to be doing what we are doing . . . as well as look at whether we are being martyrs who work long hours because it makes us feel that we are somehow doing our jobs to a deeper extent than others. What we do know, besides the self-induced issues we may face in our daily practices, is that there are demands put on teachers and school leaders that cause them to be reactive as opposed to proactive. . . . This has become a crisis in schools that we need to address. (para. 3)

He goes on to urge educators to adopt decluttering or "deimplementation"—that is, to stop current practices that have low value (Dewitt, 2021, para. 14). It is a similar concept to Marie Kondo's (2014) KonMari method of organizing and decluttering your life—a philosophy that emphasizes keeping only those things that "spark joy" and discarding items that no longer serve a purpose or bring happiness.

DeWitt notes that decluttering requires taking a long hard look at what we do:

> One of the issues I find is that people often want to get rid of what they believe is imposed on them as opposed to looking within their own practices to see what isn't working. If we want to get time back and ease our stress and anxiety, it means we must look at the big and small items we can deimplement. That begins with teachers and leaders taking a breath, being present in the situation, and then engaging in honest conversations about what we need to be doing in our day-to-day practices in school. (DeWitt, 2021, para. 21)

We recently ran a survey on the human side of school leadership and asked principals to identify the areas of work they spent the most time on. Given a list of activities, principals were asked to indicate their top three most time-consuming tasks. Their answers were revealing. Here are the most time-consuming types of work experienced by school leaders, as indicated by the percent of principals who selected the task as a "top three":

- 73%: Performing internal administrative tasks (e.g., budgets, reports, timetables)
- 45%: Communicating with people (staff, students, school community)
- 41%: Responding to crises/unexpected events
- 32%: Responding to directives from government departments/agencies
- 27%: Raising the quality of teaching and learning

If you had to guess, how much time do you spend across these five categories? If you are like many education leaders, you want to spend your time doing strategic work to improve the quality of teaching and learning—but you likely end up filling your days with more mundane administrative tasks. With so much work to be done, it's an easy trap to fall into.

Years ago, Steven Covey (n.d.) shared a helpful analogy using rocks and pebbles in a jar. He started with a jar mostly filled with pebbles and then asked people to put large rocks in the jar, which as you can imagine was nearly impossible. The only way to get everything to fit was to place the large rocks in the jar first. With the biggest rocks in the jar, the pebbles all easily fit into the spaces between. Covey's analogy is clear. If you prioritize the most important things first, everything else will fall into place around them; however, if you let your time be taken up with minutiae, you will never get to the big rocks.

Stephen, the administrator from the beginning of this chapter, had to declutter his previous practice in order to find time for the big rocks that felt most important: bringing principals and key stakeholders together to collaboratively create a townwide shared vision for school improvement. He realized how empowering this would be for principals and teachers alike and how it could help schools make sense of all the new policies and programs being rolled out by the state department of education. However, he couldn't do this without letting something go, so, buoyed by the fresh start that every new year brings, he took a long hard look at his regular diary commitments and questioned the length and frequency of every meeting. He delegated less critical duties and took the bold step of not acting at all on some trivial jobs he'd always done without thinking. This created the time and space Stephen needed to do things differently, and the impact he had on student achievement was huge.

A school leader recently shared this key challenge with one of our coaches: "I would like to be more mindful of taking a breath to identify a better way to figure out what projects or problems to tackle first." In response, the coach helped this leader prioritize using the Eisenhower Prioritization Matrix.

The Eisenhower Prioritization Matrix was popularized from a quote often attributed to Dwight D. Eisenhower: "I have two kinds of problems, the urgent and the important. The urgent are not important, and the important are never urgent." President Eisenhower never claimed that this was his own insight; he attributed it to an unnamed college president. Regardless of its origin, the matrix (Figure 5.2) is a helpful tool to prioritize your work.

FIGURE 5.2
Eisenhower Prioritization Matrix

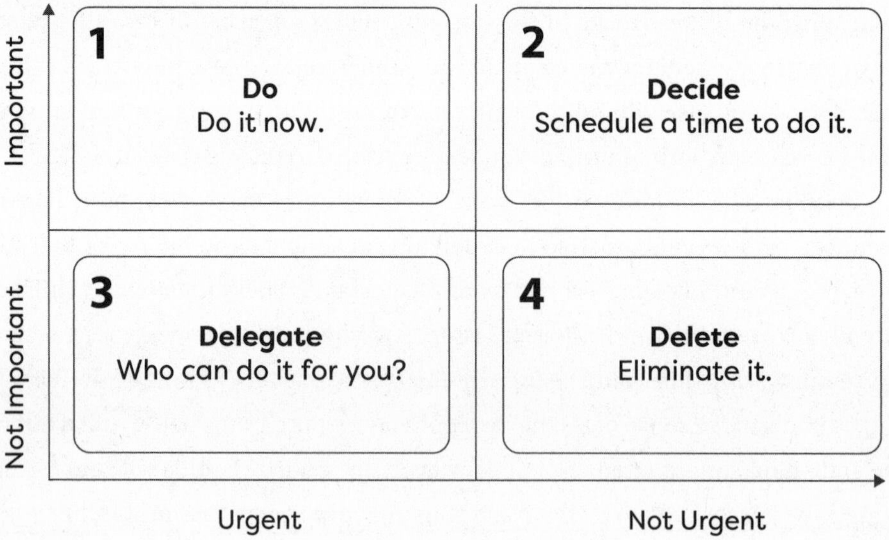

The Eisenhower Prioritization Matrix consists of four quadrants:

- **Quadrant 1:** Urgent and important items. These tasks have important deadlines or might be a crisis you must respond to now. You need to **do** these items.
- **Quadrant 2:** Not urgent but important items. These tasks are important, but you can **decide** when they need to get done. You can schedule these items and plan for longer term development.
- **Quadrant 3:** Urgent but not important items. These tasks must be done and have deadlines, but they aren't that important. They are distractions from the more important work you should be doing. These are perfect tasks for you to **delegate**. Who can do it for you?
- **Quadrant 4:** Not urgent and not important items. These tasks are complete distractions. They aren't necessary and can be eliminated from your to-do list. Therefore, go ahead and **delete** them.

When you segment your to-do items into these quadrants, you immediately have a series of quick wins. Your list will get shorter as you cross off those items in Quadrant 4. Your time will be further freed up as you allocate the Quadrant 3 items to others (who may even benefit from the opportunity to extend their skills). You are now ready to allocate your time to the important items in Quadrants 1 and 2. Of course, you'll need to prioritize items in Quadrant 1 first. Once you've tackled the urgent and important tasks, most of your time should be spent on items in Quadrant 2.

> *"I've found the Eisenhower Prioritization Matrix quite empowering. Rather than being paralyzed by the immensity of what is in front of me, it enables me to act."*

After trying out the Eisenhower Prioritization Matrix, one principal shared how useful it was to view their to-do list through a new lens: "As the leader of a small school, I wear a lot of hats. I must get better at prioritizing and seeing how things overlap, or I'll never get anything done. The matrix helped me sort my tasks. It assisted me in seeing how important some things I was doing were and why it mattered to devote time to them." Managing your time in a more conscious way can reap huge benefits—for your personal effectiveness as a leader, the impact you have on your school, and your own sense of well-being. The unfortunate reality is that too many leaders spend most of their time focused on Quadrants 3 and 4. They are busy and accomplishing things, but they are accomplishing things of little importance.

In our coaching work, we've also found that teams can get caught up in the same traps. One department head realized that her team meetings tended to start with getting some so-called little things out of the way, but they would end up taking more time than expected and the larger issues wouldn't get the attention they needed. She used the Eisenhower Prioritization Matrix to help her team organize their meeting agendas differently.

Recognizing That Old Habits Die Hard

Seizing momentum requires a different way of working, but old habits die hard. After a lifetime of procrastination, it may be second nature to be reactive rather than proactive. Changing that mindset isn't easy, but it is possible! A school leader shared, "It was a new insight for me that I can create more capacity in my day by changing the way I do things." Prioritizing means giving up on the urge to simply check things off a list in a never-ending quest to feel productive.

If you're wondering how you can truly change your work practices, it may be helpful to consider the pushes and pulls of change (Figure 5.3). On the right-hand side of this model, you can see that you need to be crystal clear about your goal (the positive change you want to make) so it can push you along through the tough times. Likewise, you need to be equally aware of the chains that hold you back. It's critical to have that self-awareness around your behaviors that may prevent you from making the change you are seeking—and where they stem from.

FIGURE 5.3
The Push and Pull of Change

Pull	Push
The chains that hold you back	**The positive change you want to make**
1. What is the most important behavior that goes against the outcome you want?	1. What outcome would you like to have?
2. There's a reason you are doing this counterproductive behavior. What self-talk shows up when you think about NOT doing it?	2. What is important to you about this?
3. What's the payoff/value/need of this behavior? What alternative behavior will meet this payoff that aligns with your positive change?	3. What are some of the behaviors you would be doing if you had already made this change?

For example, one principal in a large school knew that he needed to delegate more to others on the senior leadership team. He was shouldering too much, anxious to protect colleagues who were all busy, and fearful that they may not do things to the same high standard that he set for himself. His coach helped him articulate the push of change: improve his personal well-being and achieve his big vision (create a continuous improvement culture where leadership is shared and all staff feel empowered). Getting clearer on this *why* helped him recognize and tackle the chains that were inevitably pulling him back to old ways of working: his natural tendency to be a martyr and his anxiety that others would let him down and he would have to pick up the pieces. Once these pushes and pulls were identified, the principal was struck by the realization that he wasn't being fair on himself: "We think so often about the workload for our staff teams without considering the workload for ourselves."

When working through the pushes and pulls of change, coaching support can make a big difference to your long-term chances of success. Figure 5.4 shows a

FIGURE 5.4
Example of a Coaching Objective for Seizing Momentum

My coaching objective: I'd like to create more capacity in my day by changing the way I do things, making time to consider what is next, and seeing other ways of doing things.	
From (my current reality)	**To (my goal)**
• I like people to think that I work hard and do a good job. • If I ever sit still at work, it worries me. • I don't want people to think I'm not busy. I live very much in the moment. • If I do the work myself, I'm in control of when it gets done and the quality of the work. • If I'm busy taking care of things, I can put off other work I'm not very good at like visioning or creating a detailed implementation plan.	• It's OK for people to see me being still. I don't need to be dashing about all the time to be working hard. • I will have a clear view of where each of the strands of what I'm doing is going. • I will make time to consider what is next and see other ways of doing things. • I will put myself into uncomfortable positions—for example, visiting other schools for comparison. I will stress test what I'm doing. I will step out of my comfort zone. • I will give tasks to others when appropriate. • I will use time deliberately, with thought about the best use of my time. I will take time to reflect.

coaching objective set by a school leader who was aiming to seize momentum. Prior to beginning coaching, this leader shared, "I think and act very quickly as there is so much to be done. I make decisions quickly but then don't always feel confident that they are the right decisions. I wonder what my leadership would look like if I had more time."

You may not have access to a coach right now. Nevertheless, there is something powerful in writing down a personal objective. Committing it to paper means it is less liable to get lost in the busyness of your mind—and of course you can always refer to it later and reflect on your progress.

Seizing momentum as a school leader requires personal agency; it means taking back control. It requires a commitment to recalibrate your time, understand what might be holding you back, and take proactive actions. Stephen could have easily moved into victim mode after his department of education decided to halt the school amalgamation; instead, he seized momentum, co-created a townwide vision for education, and used this as a north star to interpret and implement all future policy directives. Likewise, Leslie rekindled her passion for work when she found a way to get involved in strengthening teaching and learning in classrooms. Even without a coach, you can begin by reflecting on how you manage your time and creating a from/to aspirational vision for yourself and your own practice.

One school leader summed this up beautifully: "The good news is that we don't need to work harder or longer. We just need to be proactive and focus on the right work. I realized that I need to (a) stop procrastinating, (b) prioritize what is most important, and (c) stop being busy!"

Go Do

No matter how many educational theories we understand or how much advice we take on as leaders, experimenting and implementing new behaviors on the job is the only thing that will change our practice. Here are some ideas to help you become a leader who is able to seize momentum:

1. Track where your tasks fall on the Eisenhower Prioritization Matrix over the course of a week. At the end of the week, reflect:
   a. What trends do you notice?
   b. What are your patterns of avoidance? What proactivity strategies or mitigation strategies for procrastination can you leverage to better get things done?
2. Draft a personal objective to frame the shift you would like to make in your own practice with respect to seizing momentum. This could relate to one of the three *P*s (proactivity, procrastination, prioritization). Identify a concrete action you can take in the next two weeks to help you make progress toward this.

Reflection Questions

- Which of the three *P*s (proactivity, procrastination, prioritization) is most important for you to address to enhance your effectiveness at work?
- What are your key insights from this chapter?
- How could you use this chapter's MESSY tools to ensure that you seize momentum to make progress toward your vision?
- Which go-do activity will you experiment with?

6

Y for Your Presence

Key Challenge: What kind of leader is most effective today?

Uncommon Sense: We think people want strong leaders, but people often thrive most when leaders are simply authentic, open, and self-aware.

Tony, a principal of a large high school, had been in his role for a few years when he suffered a crisis of confidence. He had experienced some real wins as principal—the parent community respected him, student achievement scores had improved, and new electives had been added to the course selection. Nevertheless, he was exhausted from years of feeling like he had to put a mask on every day at school. He was trying too hard to be the stereotypical superhero principal, endlessly cheerful, utterly dedicated, and all-knowing. The reality was that, despite his efforts, he was still struggling with a few very senior teachers who were resistant to implementing any new school improvement strategies. They would nod and agree with plans in faculty meetings but then sabotage Tony's efforts behind his back with less senior teachers.

Tony, who was usually very forthright with people, felt his confidence wane, especially when he had to have difficult conversations or call people out on their behavior. He vacillated between overstating his case to prove he was right and avoiding interactions with the resistant senior teachers altogether. However, the more he avoided them, the more he felt his confidence dip. Tony recognized that even though he was skilled at building relationships with people he got along with, he was much less confident with people he didn't get along with. He also had an underlying fear of failure and "not getting it right" that increased even more as his confidence decreased.

Tony's coach worked with him to revisit and analyze his values and help him reaffirm that student success was clearly his goal. His purpose as a principal wasn't to be liked by everyone. This awareness emboldened him to push forward with change initiatives despite the resistance of a few teachers. With his coach, Tony reviewed some key leadership strategies they'd discussed in their coaching conversations: the Presence Triangle, A FIRM feedback, and the Breakthrough Thinking Cycle (one of the teachers was stuck in a thinking trap).

Through this work, Tony was able to identify the assumptions he held about himself and others—especially assumptions he had about the resistant teachers and why they might be resisting change. He saw the need to park his current approach with these teachers and try something else. He slowed down and recognized how impatient he had been previously, and he became more curious and open. Rather than writing off the resistant teachers or feeling threatened by them, Tony started viewing things from their perspectives and could see the questions they raised as legitimate concerns rather than personal attacks on his leadership and strategy.

As a result, Tony shifted his anxieties and started to feel a newfound confidence. He discovered the importance of checking his own self-talk and adding *yet* to some sentences, giving himself the time and space to learn and grow as a leader. These shifts helped him feel more satisfied in his job since he was able to align his actions with his values, operate more strategically, and feel that he wasn't continually failing in his role.

Tony made a self-proclaimed shift from trying to be a principal superhero to being a wise person who was still growing and learning. This critical leadership shift is in many ways the most important of the MESSY model, and it goes deep and personal into your presence.

Your presence is a shift from a mindset of "I struggle with the superhero syndrome, portraying strength and expertise, even when I feel weak and uncertain" to one of "I own who I am as a leader—my strengths and my shortcomings. I am willing to be curious, be humble, and learn."

Even during the best of times, working in schools can be very demanding, requiring educators to balance different and often competing needs and continuously make tough decisions. Over time, this can cause us to question our own capabilities and create self-doubt. Recall the Me Us It model of leadership from Chapter 1. The *me* is a focus on ourselves, our attitudes, and our behaviors; the *us* is a focus on our relationships and interactions with others; and the *it* is a focus on our work and the tasks involved. This chapter will focus on the *me* part of the model—the part that often gets left out or ignored altogether.

How MESSY Are You?

Before diving further into your presence, take a few minutes to reflect on your own leadership. How comfortable are you as a leader? Are you aware of your leadership presence and how that influences your work? Where would you rate yourself on the Your Presence MESSY Monitor (Figure 6.1)? Where might a close colleague or friend rate you? (An aggregate rubric, which combines each chapter's MESSY leadership monitor, can be found in Appendix A.)

If you found yourself selecting *Frequently* or *Very Often*, then these are likely areas of strength for you. However, if you found yourself selecting *Never* or *Rarely* on some of the items, then these are probably areas of struggle for you. The strategies and tools (In and Out of the Box, Mindtraps, Emotion Truth

FIGURE 6.1
Your Presence MESSY Monitor

Your Presence Behaviors	Never	Rarely	Sometimes	Frequently	Very Often
I am aware of my emotional state and how it affects my leadership.					
I can deliberately manage my state and choose how I respond to challenges.					
I recognize when I am not at my best and the impact it has on me, others, and my work.					
I am confident in my leadership capabilities.					
I feel comfortable being myself in my leadership role.					
I know my native genius and can leverage it in how I lead.					
I am intellectually curious.					

Choice) shared in this chapter are designed to support you in building your capabilities to build up your presence.

Building Your Sense of Confidence

Tony isn't alone in feeling a lack of confidence, despite advanced degrees, credentials, years of experience, and success. There seems to be a universal mental picture of what an effective school leader looks like. They are typically seen as being confident, having all the answers, meeting everyone's needs, and solving all the problems. Indeed, this stereotypical school leader image can cause you to question your own skills, experience, and value.

In coaching sessions with school leaders, confidence comes up time and time again as an area with which leaders want more support. In our research, we found confidence, authority, and imposter syndrome to be recurring themes for leaders. This holds true regardless of the seniority level or years of experience—from new team leader to superintendent. As one of our coaches noted, "Too often, school leaders come in with extensive expertise, yet many still suffer from imposter syndrome. A lot of my time is about helping leaders own who they are and feel more confident in their ability to do the job."

> *"My coaching shift: to feel confident and show up, stand up, and say, 'Here I am!'"*

Confidence can be defined as a belief in one's abilities, qualities, and judgments. It refers to the level of assurance or trust that an individual has in their own capabilities to succeed in a particular situation or achieve a specific goal. People who are confident tend to be more successful in their personal and professional lives; they are more likely to take risks, pursue their goals, and handle setbacks and failures with resilience and determination.

How confident do you feel with your leadership presence? Take a moment to reflect on these common scenarios and determine where you feel most confident and least confident:

- Presenting in front of others.
- Analyzing student achievement data.
- Being expected to be innovative or creative.
- Engaging in difficult or challenging conversations.
- Working with tight deadlines.
- Learning new skills.
- Taking on a new role or responsibility.
- Speaking to more senior leaders.

Perhaps other situations specific to your role and position come to mind. The goal here is to create more self-awareness about your confidence levels in different situations. With the insight gained from your reflection, you can start to build on your strengths and identify specific situations where you want to improve your confidence.

There are a lot of myths around confidence (e.g., people are born with confidence, confidence comes with success), so let's clarify three truths:

1. It's completely normal to feel like an imposter or have doubt.
2. Success is more about the things you do than your confidence level while doing them.
3. It's authentic to be uncomfortable with the unknown.

A lack of confidence is a mindset that is not a direct reflection of one's ability, potential outcomes, or chances of success. Leaders who experience a lack of confidence or impostor syndrome feel like they don't belong or that they're not good enough for their job. They often fear being exposed as a fraud. They feel like they must work harder than others to prove themselves, and they may struggle with feelings of guilt or shame for not living up to expectations. In reality, lack of confidence has much more to do with your own perception of yourself.

Knowing that this is a mindset means this insight can be utilized to build a more confident mindset. You can learn to project authentic confidence by drawing on four sources: (1) expertise and credibility; (2) personal experience and perspective; (3) character, strengths, and presence; and (4) values and beliefs. As you read through these sources of authentic confidence, jot down what comes to mind for each category. Your own list of sources can be a great list to pull out when you are feeling unsure or when you could use a boost of confidence.

Expertise and credibility. Confidence can come from feeling skilled or knowledgeable in a particular area. For example, the degrees and credentials you hold may increase your confidence in handling related situations. The different types of leadership positions you have had—or how long you have been in those positions—can add to your credibility.

Personal experience and perspective. Confidence can also come from past experiences, particularly those in which you have succeeded. If you have overcome challenges or achieved goals in the past, you may feel more confident in your ability to do so again in the future. These are the highlights and successes you've experienced in your leadership career.

Character, strengths, and presence. Your character, strengths, and presence help others perceive confidence in you. Authentic confidence also comes from a deep understanding of your strengths and weaknesses. When you are aware of your own capabilities and limitations, you can better navigate situations that may challenge you. Liz Wiseman (2017) suggests that all leaders identify and tap into their native genius, which she defines as a skill that comes naturally, easily, and freely. If you don't already know what your native genius is, try asking yourself these questions: "What do I do better than anything else? What do I do better than the people around me? What do I do easily (without effort or even awareness)? What do I do freely (without being asked or even paid)?" Once you have identified your native genius, you can leverage it in the work you do.

Values and beliefs. Your strength of purpose can give you authority and authenticity. Others like to follow leaders with a strong set of core values, and their loyalty can help give you confidence in yourself. One's values can provide a sense of purpose, meaning, and direction in life, which can in turn lead to a greater sense of self-worth and confidence. When someone lives in alignment with their values, they feel more authentic and truer to themselves, which can help them feel more confident in their decisions and actions.

Take a moment to reflect on which of these sources of authentic confidence you could draw on, especially during times of self-doubt. Authentic confidence is different from arrogance or overconfidence, which can be detrimental to personal and professional growth. Authentic confidence is based on a realistic understanding of yourself and your abilities. Although it's completely normal to feel like an imposter or let doubt creep in, try tapping into your sources of authentic confidence in situations where you feel unsure.

Becoming More Self-Aware

Many school leaders have become accustomed to putting themselves last in service of others. In fact, putting yourself last may even be an unwritten expectation that you hold for yourself—or that you feel your community holds for you. One principal told her coach, "I felt like I had to be the first one on campus every day and the last one to leave. It was a great goal, but it wasn't sustainable or even healthy for me in the long term."

When asked about how they begin their workday, many school leaders share that from the moment they get to work, they are rushing to complete tasks, solve problems for others, and put out fires without giving much thought to setting their day up for success. They are unintentionally trying to be everyone's superhero. In this sense, leaders might be surviving, but by ignoring their own needs, they aren't thriving. As they continue to neglect themselves over the course of years, their unmet personal needs may end up surfacing in other ways. They may become irritable, start procrastinating, or are no longer able to show up as their best selves, which then negatively affects school climate and culture.

It doesn't have to be this way. You are good enough as you are, and with a few simple tools, you can be more confident in how you show up as a leader and in establishing boundaries that will help you thrive over the long term. As one leader shared, "I now see I must put on my own 'oxygen mask' first so I can be effective for staff and students." An important step in developing your presence is to bring the *me* into balance by better understanding how to manage your own emotional state and resourcefulness. As simple as it sounds, this work begins with self-awareness.

> *"Less stress is not only possible, it is something I can choose."*

Take a moment and reflect on two recent situations.

First, think about a time when you were at your very best—a moment when you showed up in a way that makes you feel proud. Your scenario could be at work, but it could also be with your family or friends. Now bring that moment clearly to mind and imagine stepping right back into that moment as if you were reliving it. Reflect, "What do I feel in my body? What am I thinking right now? What am I saying to myself?" It can be powerful to relive such positive experiences. We call them anchor moments.

Now take a deep breath and think back to a time when you weren't at your best—a moment when you didn't handle a situation well. You might even be embarrassed to recall this time. As before, try to get a vivid mental image of that moment: where you were, what you were doing, what triggered your reaction. Then imagine stepping right back into that moment, reliving it all again. What are you feeling? What are you thinking? What are you saying to yourself? It probably doesn't feel at all comfortable going back to that moment, but you can learn a lot from becoming more aware of your thoughts and feelings in those challenging moments.

These two situations likely triggered different emotional responses for you. We use the terms *in the box* and *out of the box* (Figure 6.2) to describe these two very different states. When you're not at your best, you are highjacked by your feelings—unhappiness, self-doubt, defensiveness, or pessimism. Your self-talk is often negative, and these negative thought patterns keep you in a negative place. We refer to this as *in the box* because you tend to feel constrained and unresourceful.

FIGURE 6.2
In the Box Versus Out of the Box

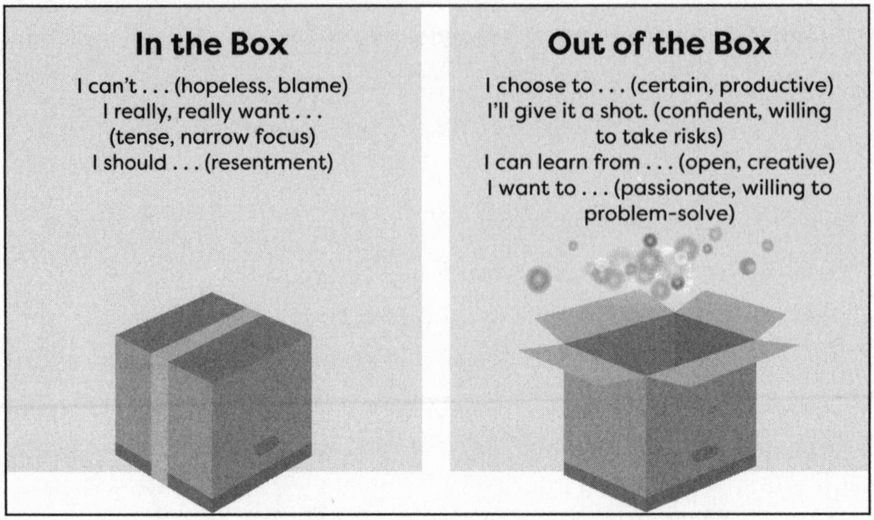

In the Box
I can't . . . (hopeless, blame)
I really, really want . . . (tense, narrow focus)
I should . . . (resentment)
Out of the Box
I choose to . . . (certain, productive)
I'll give it a shot. (confident, willing to take risks)
I can learn from . . . (open, creative)
I want to . . . (passionate, willing to problem-solve)

On the other hand, when you're operating as the best version of yourself, your feelings and self-talk are generative—they inform you of your choices and help you learn, build confidence, see opportunities, and take risks. We refer to this state as *out of the box*. When you are at your best, you are likely experiencing feelings such as happiness, confidence, hope, optimism, and enthusiasm.

Most of us experience a roller coaster ride each day, oscillating between feeling positive and capable and feeling negative or uncertain. That's completely normal. The trick is to be able to recognize when you are not at your best—when you're in the box—and build a toolkit for learning to get out of the box. Why is this so important? If you need to suddenly respond to something at school, you will be far more effective if you are out of the box. Depending on what state of mind you are in, your response and therefore your impact will be very different. How you are feeling affects your thinking and therefore your actions.

> *"Don't be hijacked by your thoughts and feelings!"*

Often, the hardest part is to recognize that you are in the box to begin with. It's easier to recognize when you are stressed, but also look for times when you are feeling a bit flat, uninspired, or even on autopilot from trying to do too much. These are all emotions that are likely indicators of being in the box.

By being aware of negative self-talk and how you feel, you can learn what types of situations trigger you to go in the box. This is created by stress hormones when you react to a trigger or perceived threat. Your triggers can come from anywhere—an email from a parent, a request from the district office, or a request to cover another class when the substitute doesn't show. Take a minute to think about what triggers you to go in the box. Whatever your triggers are, they cause your brain to release a cocktail of chemicals that essentially shuts down your rational brain and distorts your thinking. When this happens, you're no longer thinking rationally, you're reacting, which in turn affects your behavior—how you respond, the impact you have on others, and the results you get.

What triggers you to go in the box? What impact does this have on you, the people around you, and your ability to do your job? Showing up as less than your best self because you are in the box is a syndrome of the *brain*, but the cure to get out of the box starts with the *heart*. The first thing to focus on is not how you are *thinking* but what you are *feeling*. Dan Siegel, author of many books on emotional intelligence, shares research that shows that by both recognizing and specifically naming our emotions, we lessen the power and impact of these emotions. Siegel (2021) calls this the "name it to tame it" theory. Although this sounds simple, you are likely guilty of denying or repressing your emotions or of indulging and being victim to your emotions. When you are in the box, it profoundly affects how you see and interact with the world. Being emotional is human, but by being informed of your feelings, you create the opportunity to choose your response rather than just react.

These emotions tend to distort our thinking; they distort how we perceive and interpret reality. Whether you realize it or not, you have two inner voices that often characterize being in the box: the judge and the pessimist (see Figure 6.3). The judge makes broad, sweeping judgments about the situation or people involved. This could include both judgments aimed outward (at others) and inward (at yourself). The judge might say things like "You don't know what

FIGURE 6.3
Your Inner Voices

Judge:
Makes judgments about ourselves and/or about others.
Pessimist: Imagines the worst, picturing the potential negatives.
Realist:
Is wise and tells the truth.

you are doing" or "That is a terrible idea!" By contrast, the pessimist focuses on the downsides of any given situation. It immediately sees problems and might say things like "Nothing I do will make a difference" or "That will never work!" Your goal is to silence these two voices and amplify the voice of the realist: the wise, rational self that can accurately perceive and honestly interpret reality. This is the voice that helps you show up as your best self in every situation.

Understanding How Self-Talk Influences Effectiveness

Learning what triggers you to be in the box—and which strategies can get you out of the box—requires self-awareness and practice. Everyone is unique, but there are a few common mindtraps that often hold people in the box. Mindtraps are the unproductive inner thoughts or self-talk that distort the reality of a situation, causing you to jump to conclusions or assume the worst. These mindtraps limit your ability to be the best leader possible. By understanding which mindtraps catch you most often, as well as their impact on others and your work, you can better respond to triggering situations and learn how to rebound more quickly.

Take a few minutes to complete the mindtraps questionnaire in Figure 6.4. We all fall for mindtraps and likely experience many within the course of a single day. The six mindtraps can be separated into two broad groups: judging mindtraps and pessimist mindtraps.

FIGURE 6.4
Mindtraps Questionnaire

Answer the following questions about yourself, using these scores:

1: Regularly (i.e., 2–3 times per month)
½: Occasionally
0: Rarely

A. When you are not at your best, do you . . .

Assume others will judge you by your achievements, comparing you to your peers and people in positions superior to you?	
Succeed at something and then move on to the next thing with little celebration?	
Find that, given your drive to achieve, you find it frustrating having to spend time consulting with and listening to others (especially if you don't value their opinion)?	
Not feel satisfied with your achievements, even though you have reached certain goals you set for yourself?	
Become self-critical when things don't turn out the way you want?	
TOTAL	

B. When you are not at your best, do you . . .

Censor or edit what you say in certain meetings?	
Hold back when you would like to put yourself forward?	
See a particular individual's shortcomings more easily than their strengths?	
Set high standards and criticize yourself and others if you fail to meet them?	
Feel judgmental of yourself or others?	
TOTAL	

C. When you are not at your best, do you . . .

Worry about what others think of you?	
Agree to something that, upon reflection, you had rather you did not?	
Become anxious (and perhaps a little vague in your language) when conflict is likely?	
Go out of your way to accommodate others' needs (even when it seems to be taken for granted)?	
Feel overly concerned about upsetting others?	
TOTAL	

(continued)

FIGURE 6.4 *(Continued)*

D. When you are not at your best, do you . . .

Overplan—or feel reluctant to delegate—because you are overly focused on the downsides?	
Create unnecessary stress by imagining worst-case scenarios and potential downsides?	
Avoid taking a course of action you imagine might be risky (but later wished you'd gone with)?	
Make a mistake and dwell on its implications?	
Take a long time to make decisions (worrying that you might have missed something)?	
TOTAL	

E. When you are not at your best, do you . . .

Think there is nothing you can do about . . . ?	
Think you have too much going on and no time to do what is needed?	
Think that your organization/project/boss prevents you from performing the way you could or achieving your goals?	
Have good intentions or goals but can't quite get around to making them happen?	
Find it easier to see faults in others than yourself?	
TOTAL	

F. When you are not at your best, do you . . .

Put off the things you love to do in favor of getting the job under control?	
Put up with things or tasks you disagree with or disapprove of?	
Put your team, family, and/or job ahead of your own needs?	
Tend to overprotect others rather than let them see the full consequences of a situation?	
Lose the fun at work?	
TOTAL	

Once you've completed the Mindtraps Questionnaire, you can use the totals to learn about the mindtraps you are most likely to experience. The sections with the higher total scores are the ones to pay attention to, as they are ones that can trip you up the most. Don't be alarmed if you have several of these; this is quite normal! You may want to revisit this questionnaire another time. Leadership is contextual, so what trips us up can change depending on the context.

Mindtraps Scoring Totals	
Section A: *Prover*	
Section B: *Critic/Doubter*	
Section C: *Pleaser*	
Section D: *Worrier*	
Section E: *Victim/Avoider*	
Section F: *Martyr*	

Judging Mindtraps

Prover: Leaders struggling with the prover mindtrap need to see themselves as continually successful. They don't leave any room for failure. This belief causes leaders to always prove they are right, and they need to do everything perfectly. Constantly striving for perfection rarely lets them celebrate success because they quickly focus all their energy on the next goal. Provers can quickly become task-focused and find it difficult to listen to and engage noncontributors. *"I used to believe I had to be perfect. I now see the perfection in imperfection."*

Critic/Doubter: This mindtrap centers on the belief that there is always room for improvement to a fault. These leaders constantly question their own strengths and capabilities and the ability of others. Therefore, when things don't work out, they point blame at themselves or others. They can be distrustful and are rarely satisfied, even if they achieve their goal. *"I need to stop questioning my own qualifications for my role. I am not an accidental principal; I am qualified and deserve to be here."*

Pleaser: The pleaser mindtrap focuses on likability. We find this to be a very common mindtrap among school leaders. Pleasers want to be liked by everyone and believe harmony is more important than conflict. Therefore, pleasers act in order to please others, have a hard time saying no or establishing boundaries, and avoid conflict at all costs. Focusing on others' perceptions often results in a form of leadership that avoids conflict or lacks backbone. *"I just want to have a good relationship with everyone, but I'm slowly realizing that I can't keep everyone happy all the time."*

Pessimist Mindtraps

Worrier: The worrier mindtrap causes leaders to see the future as bleak and feel that things tend to always go wrong. Therefore, the worrier will do everything in their power to mitigate risks or avoid taking risks at all. They waste valuable time and energy overthinking potential negative scenarios. Worrying about the consequences of an action means leadership can be cautious or lack conviction.

"Historically, the achievement data for my school has not been strong. I couldn't help but worry about the students we've failed, but now I see that was keeping me from acting in the best interest of the current students we have right now."

Victim/Avoider: The biggest belief associated with the victim/avoider mindtrap is a sense of helplessness. Leaders struggling with this mindtrap may feel that they can't do anything about the way things are or that it's not their job to do something about it. For example, it can be easy for those in schools to feel like victims when they need to enact yet another district-mandated policy. These beliefs lead to inaction and complaints about why others don't fix things. Leaders experiencing this mindtrap let situations get worse and only face them when forced to. They may shut down options ("That will never work"), shift the blame ("That's his job"), or never even get round to solving a particularly thorny issue. *"I tend to get caught up in finding faults in the wider education system—government policy, those in district office—and arguing that nothing I do at the school level will make much of a difference. I see now that I use these things as an excuse to not act."*

Martyr: Those struggling with the martyr mindtrap believe that if they don't take on a task (whatever it may be), then no one will. Martyrs believe that they are putting others first for the sake of the greater good, without realizing the personal toll it takes on them. They will do what they are supposed to do, and what they feel is right, often putting themselves second, but they then feel resentful about the work they have done. These leaders often end up doing something because they think they ought to or should. They tend to take on too much and their leadership ends up lacking passion and commitment. *"I know I fall into the martyr mindtrap, yet I don't fully reflect on the personal toll and the toll it has on my leadership. I need to learn to chill out, get rid of 'should,' and share the load more."*

Your Mindtraps

Which mindtrap resonates most with you? If more than one resonates, rest assured that you are not alone! For example, earlier in this chapter, we looked at the issue of confidence. A lack of confidence can stem from being too harsh on yourself (critic/doubter), trying to keep everyone happy (pleaser), fearing failure (prover), or imagining the worst (worrier)—or any combination of these!

Like many school leaders, Tony realized he was experiencing a real medley of mindtraps. As he worked to improve his confidence, he could see that his natural tendency to be a pleaser meant he wasn't tackling issues head-on with his uncooperative teachers; he often avoided difficult conversations. He was also falling victim to the critic/doubter mindtrap, being too harsh on himself (for not being an "effective principal") and others (not taking the time to understand why they were struggling to embrace and implement new initiatives). His efforts to be a superhero principal tended to result in him spending more and more time in martyr mode, taking on the brunt of school improvement work himself in order to avoid overburdening his leadership team. Recognizing these mindtraps helped Tony see that he would be more successful if he took a more strengths-based approach and focused on individuals' strengths rather than their shortcomings. He also didn't have to do this alone; he could share leadership more effectively with his assistant principals.

We have found that the two most common mindtraps for educators are the pleaser and the martyr. One reason for this could be the pressure and expectations placed on school leaders to meet the needs and demands of various stakeholders. To please everyone and maintain positive relationships, leaders may end up prioritizing the needs of others over their own well-being. Additionally, school leaders may feel a strong sense of responsibility for the success of their students and staff, leading them to sacrifice their own needs for the benefit of others—and be the superhero leader.

It's interesting to note that mindtraps can be a distortion of a core quality that really matters to you. For example, someone who is a strong pleaser will, at their best, be great at building trusting relationships since they are driven by empathy and care. However, when their pleaser mindtrap becomes triggered, they find themselves avoiding addressing poor behavior or lacking leadership backbone since they are overconcerned with keeping everyone happy. In this case, the core

FIGURE 6.5
The Core Qualities and Feelings Behind Mindtraps

Mindtrap	Feelings	Core Qualities
Pleaser	resentment, low-grade anxiety, apprehension, guilt	empathy, care
Critic/Doubter	frustration, anger, self-doubt, helplessness, stress	humility, discernment, good judgment, honesty
Prover	adrenalin-fueled excitement, tense driven energy, stress	ambition, drive
Worrier	anxiety, fear	concern, conscientiousness
Victim/Avoider	hopelessness, anxiety, exasperation	self-care, self-preservation
Martyr	resentment, irritation, apathy	responsibility, care

qualities of empathy and care are being overplayed. Figure 6.5 lists the mindtraps with examples of their core qualities.

As you reflect on your own leadership, consider what qualities sit alongside your mindtraps. Can you imagine how you could hold on to this important quality and yet not allow it to become so strong that it triggers a mindtrap?

Getting Out of the Box to Regain Your Leadership Effectiveness

We know every leader can be triggered and eventually falls prey to a mindtrap, so we want to give you a tool that can help you break free from your negative self-talk and instead be more choiceful in how you respond to a situation. Emotion Truth Choice (ETC, see Figure 6.6) is a tool you can use to help break free from the exaggerated pessimistic and judging thoughts you experience. The best way to learn the ETC process is to apply it to an issue you've recently encountered, one that put you in the box, and work through the steps relevant to that issue. At its simplest level, ETC is about three things: (1) recognizing your emotions, (2) telling yourself the truth of the situation, and (3) making a conscious choice about how you will respond.

FIGURE 6.6
Emotion Truth Choice (ETC)

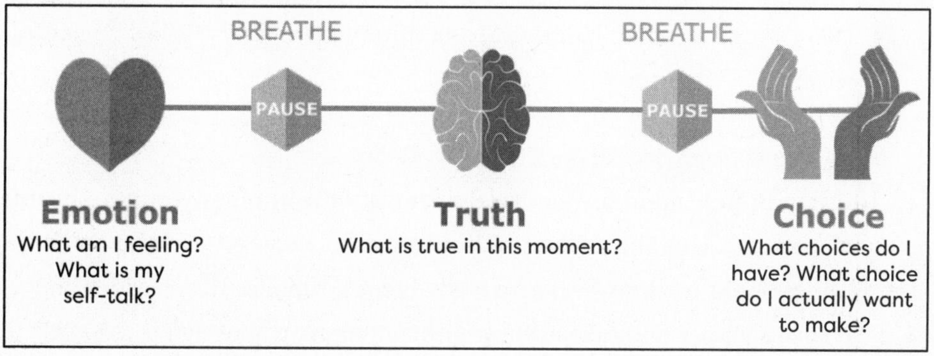

Earlier in this chapter, you identified a time when you were not at your best. Take a few minutes now to recall that moment—just after you had been triggered. Imagine yourself in that moment now, and work your way through the ETC process.

Emotion: Start with the heart. "Name and tame" the feelings you are experiencing. Don't skimp here; really do an inventory of your emotions and emotionally driven thoughts, especially those coming from the judge and pessimist voices. Try journaling your responses to these prompts:

- How are you feeling?
- What are your physiological responses?
- What is your self-talk saying? Which mindtrap are you in?
- What does this mean about you?

Now take a breath or two. Let go. Relax.

Truth: Next, move to the head. To access your realist voice—your 'inner wisdom,' as it were—take yourself back to the positive anchor moment you identified earlier. Think about that time when you were operating at your best. (Connecting back to that moment experientially should help you shift your state and feel more positive.) Bring out your realist voice and state what is true in this moment.

- Review your self-talk statements, one at a time, and answer, "What is the truth about that statement now?"
- Don't worry about fully interpreting things; just name truths in a neutral way.

Now take another breath or two. Let go. Relax.

Choice: Finally, land on the hands. Identify the choices you have in this moment, and decide on the choice you want to make. Remember, doing nothing—letting the moment pass or waiting for a bit—is a valid choice. However, it's important to make a choice and take agency in the moment. Choose your response to the situation. What can you do differently in this situation or if this situation were to occur again? What action would you commit to? What have you learned?

Let's take a moment to see the ETC process in action and revisit how Tony used it to find a new approach with the resistant teachers on his team.

> **Emotion:** I'm super upset. How can two teachers undermine the work I'm leading? I know it's because they don't like me, and they probably think my ideas aren't good. They have more experience than me, so maybe I don't know what I'm doing. Now whenever I am around them, I feel like I don't know what to do. I feel anxious and uncomfortable. They will probably try to sabotage everything I do as a leader, so I might as well give up.
>
> **Truth:** There are 40 faculty members, and only two have appeared resistant. We are making progress as a school, and most teachers are supportive of our collective efforts. The few teachers who haven't implemented the strategies yet might need more time or support.
>
> **Choice:** I am going to spend time with the few teachers who haven't implemented the strategies and really listen to them and their concerns. I am going to work to understand where they are coming from, and I might learn something that will help me improve our work.

It should be evident that, once you identify the emotions and separate them from the truth, it is much easier to choose your action. ETC is a simple process, but it takes practice. You'll need to learn to recognize your state, the triggers, and the patterns of when you go in the box. Then, when you find yourself in the box, start with the heart (What am I feeling?), move to the head (What is true in this moment?), and finally land on the hands (What do I choose to do?).

> *"When I started journaling my triggers, the patterns were alarming. I used the ETC process, and it worked wonders—a game changer!"*

It's common for school leaders to feel like they have to be superheroes and take on too much to ensure the success of their school. However, this can often lead to burnout, a poor work-life balance, and an ebbing of confidence. Our hope is that, just like Tony, other school leaders can develop greater awareness of their own limitations and strengths, intentionally working to develop their leadership and shedding the image of the "perfect" school leader. This shift from a superhero mindset to a more balanced leadership style requires a willingness to let go of some control, an awareness of oneself, and the courage to recalibrate others' expectations. By doing so, school leaders can not only avoid burnout but also create a more supportive and collaborative environment for their staff and students.

Go Do

No matter how many educational theories we understand or how much advice we take on as leaders, experimenting and implementing new behaviors on the job is the only thing that will change our practice. Here are some ideas to help you become a leader who is able to prioritize developing your presence:

1. Capture your *in the box* and *out of the box* experiences over the coming week. The easiest way to accomplish this is to put a 10-minute appointment on your calendar toward the end of each day to document the relevant experiences. At the end of the week, look for patterns in triggers.

2. The next time you find yourself in the box, utilize the ETC process. See if you can silence your judge and pessimist to connect more with your realist. Make a conscious choice on your next step.
3. Take a few minutes to reflect on the Mindtraps Questionnaire. What trap is keeping you from showing up as your best self?
4. Explore your own native genius and see if you can leverage it in certain situations to elevate your confidence.

Reflection Questions

- How might you use your *in the box* and *out of the box* experiences to show up as your best self?
- What triggers you to go in the box? What impact does this have on you, the people around you, and your ability to do the job?
- What are your key insights from this chapter?
- How could you use this chapter's MESSY tools to ensure you strengthen your leadership presence?
- Which go-do activity will you experiment with?

7

Mindsets Matter

In the previous chapter, we heard how Tony, as an experienced principal, was supported by his coach to gain newfound confidence and a sense of purpose. He learned how to slow down, get curious about those who resisted change, and not take the reluctance of some teachers too personally. This is a great example of a school leader making a mindset shift, embracing new ways of thinking that then guide behaviors and leadership practice.

Throughout this book, we have uncovered the critical mindset shifts that school leaders need to make to evolve their leadership so they can confidently lead their school communities into the future. Much has been written about how school environments have become increasingly VUCA (volatile, uncertain, complex, and ambiguous). The COVID-19 pandemic was an extreme example of this, but the education landscape continues to change. Our research and data analysis of thousands of coaching conversations with school leaders over a five-year period revealed how school leadership practice is adapting—and it formed the inspiration behind the MESSY leadership model.

This model highlights five critical mindset shifts for school leaders: those centered around meaning making, emotional connection, sensing the future, seizing momentum, and your presence. For each, we have described the foundational mindset—a typical, standard worldview—and contrasted this with an elevated mindset that can serve as an aspirational worldview to embrace. A summary of these mindset shifts is shown in Figure 7.1.

We have deliberately tried to keep each of the MESSY chapters practical with easy-to-implement tools and strategies you can integrate into your everyday leadership practice in school. We hope they will widen your toolkit and give you some scaffolds to support high-quality professional conversations.

In this chapter, we look a little more deeply at the nature of mindsets and how to achieve sustained shifts. What do we mean by the term *mindset*? Mindsets are the attitudes, beliefs, and values that often subconsciously drive our behaviors.

FIGURE 7.1
Summary of MESSY Mindset Shifts

	Foundational Mindset *From . . .*	**Elevated Mindset** *To . . .*
Meaning Making	I care about providing students with a high-quality education, so I work hard at what I do.	I create a sense of shared agency and engage others in an inspiring vision.
Emotional Connection	I am focused on my relationships with my team and stakeholders.	I have the courage to build deeper and more honest relationships within my school and community.
Sensing the Future	I create strategic plans for the future of our school but feel limited by constraints.	I am energized by possibilities and run fast-cycle experiments to contribute to an ever-evolving plan for the future.
Seizing Momentum	I focus on process and attempt to "manage" a high-quality education for students.	I am clear on the difference we want to make and focus on activities that yield better outcomes.
Your Presence	I struggle with the superhero syndrome, portraying strength and expertise, even when I feel weak and uncertain.	I own who I am as a leader—my strengths and my shortcomings. I am willing to be curious, be humble, and learn.

Why are mindsets important? If we, as educational leaders, want to grow our leadership practice and be most effective in leading our school communities, then we need to let go of unhelpful leadership behaviors and embrace new ways of working. However, much of our day-to-day behavior is driven by deep-rooted attitudes, beliefs, and values: our mindsets. Mindsets drive behavior, and behavior drives impact (on those around us) and results (for our school communities). This is such a fundamental chain reaction that BTS Spark helps every school leader we coach craft their own personal coaching objective using our MBIR framework:

Mindset (attitudes, values, and beliefs)
Behavior (visibly seen by others)
Impact (on relationships)
Results (for my school)

The idea that mindset underlies behavior can be found in neuroscience (e.g., Watkins, 2013), neurolinguistic programming (e.g., Dilts, 1990), and psychology (e.g., Assagioli, 2007; Geraskov, 1994). In the words of Brené Brown (2018), "Who we are is how we lead" (p. 11). This intuitively makes sense. We know that great school leaders have great knowledge and capabilities, and they model key mindsets. In short, they need to be great instructional leaders and great leaders of people.

Let's take an example. Like many school leaders, you may have had some training on giving feedback—probably a one-day workshop or something similar. Did it change your practice? Are you now comfortable giving feedback regularly to your colleagues? We've coached thousands of school leaders who have already engaged in professional development to improve their feedback skills, yet our research has shown that giving feedback confidently is the most frequently sought mindset shift among the school leaders we coach. How can this be?

When we explore this further, people tell us that "I learned and practiced a scaffold for a feedback conversation, but I'm still really uncomfortable with even initiating a feedback conversation." The mindset that typically holds them back is a belief that feedback is essentially a bad thing. They don't like receiving it (even positive feedback makes them cringe), and they *really* don't like giving it. Our coaches help these leaders challenge their underlying beliefs about feedback—"How can new teachers grow their practice without any feedback from others? How would students perform if they didn't get regular feedback on their work?"—and come to the realization that feedback is a gift that helps people grow and develop. This entails a gradual shift over a period of time.

Identifying Key Mindsets for School Leaders

Over the previous 15 years, educational leadership academics and thought leaders have proposed critical leadership mindsets or dispositions that underpin effective educational leadership practice. Linda Kaser and Judy Halbert (2009) were early pioneers in this field, arguing that six distinct mindsets characterize the way effective school leaders operate. Namely, they are

- Motivated by intense moral purpose.
- Knowledgeable about current models of learning.
- Consistently inquiry oriented.
- Able to build trusting relationships.
- Evidence-informed.
- Able to move to wise action.

Ken Leithwood started referring to personal leadership resources (dispositions or traits) of school leaders in 2012. He reviewed the Ontario Leadership Framework, which identified three types of personal leadership resources: cognitive resources (problem-solving expertise, domain-specific knowledge), social resources (perceiving emotions, managing emotions, acting in emotionally appropriate ways), and psychological resources (optimism, self-efficacy, resilience). He also nominated two more for inclusion: proactivity and systems thinking. Reviewing these more recently, he concluded, "While further research is required, a well-defined set of cognitive, social, and psychological 'personal leadership resources' show promise of explaining a high proportion of variation in the practices enacted by school leaders" (Leithwood et al., 2020, p. 15).

Others have highlighted specific mindsets that are becoming more critical for school leaders as they need to embrace more adaptive, future-focused leadership practice. For example, Pasi Sahlberg (2021) proposes, "School leaders need to sift new ideas and approaches. What's the evidence? Is it relevant to my context?" Sahlberg suggests a new mindset: leading with small data, received through human observations, in contrast to big data. Similarly, Valerie Hannon and Anthony Mackay (2021) outline five signposts for the future of educational leadership and emphasize the need for school leaders to shift mindsets—from service manager to social entrepreneur—and adopt a collaborative approach (partnering with community stakeholders).

One of the most comprehensive leadership mindset curricula for school leaders has been developed by our own organization, BTS Spark. This was originally developed with data gathered from more than 150,000 coaching conversations with a wide variety of leaders in different contexts. We involved academic institutions such as Singapore Management University in our data analysis and then further evolved the curriculum over the past decade. Analysis of themes across this vast data set identified four broad leadership domains:

- **Be:** These are mindsets that deal with an individual's resourcefulness, confidence, and ability to stay calm and open in any situation, even in the face of challenges and potential stress.
- **Relate:** These are mindsets that deal with relationships with other people. They include building relational trust, influencing others, having difficult conversations, and empowering others.
- **Inspire:** These are mindsets that deal with direction, change, and purpose. They include leading change, building a vision, creating shared purpose, and leading during times of uncertainty.
- **Think:** These are mindsets that deal with solving problems in a new way and looking beyond the obvious. They include challenging the way things are done, innovating, experimenting, and futures thinking.

As a school leader, you will likely encounter situations that challenge you in each of the four domains: when you take on a new role and don't feel confident *(be)*, when you need to engage people you find difficult *(relate)*, when you find yourself needing to drive change *(inspire)*, and when you are tasked with a tricky school improvement issue *(think)*.

These four leadership domains are helpful in exposing school leaders to the breadth of leadership mindsets, but they are only the start. Our more comprehensive research has identified a full range of 33 leadership mindsets that underpin effective school leadership (see Figure 7.2).

Presented with this full range of leadership mindsets, you may feel excited or overwhelmed. The good news is that, as a school leader, you don't need to have mastery of everything at once. Remember the key message in Chapter 6 about your presence? You don't have to be perfect! Maybe your school context and the challenges you face this year mean that you could benefit from strengthening one particular mindset right now. That's much more achievable.

> *"I am a work in progress. There's no 'magic bullet.' I've realized that if there is something important you need to change, then you need to work on it every day."*

When we undertook our analysis of more than 6,000 coaching conversations with school leaders over the previous five years (as a precursor to authoring this book), we analyzed leaders' coaching objectives. We wanted to answer this question: Which leadership mindsets do school leaders identify as most critical for themselves to develop? No doubt, you are curious about this too.

We uncovered nine recurring mindsets when school leaders set their personal coaching objectives (Figure 7.3). Do any resonate especially for you? If you were to put your energies into evolving just one leadership mindset, which would be your priority right now, given the challenges you are facing this year in your school?

FIGURE 7.2
A Comprehensive Curriculum of 33 School Leadership Mindsets

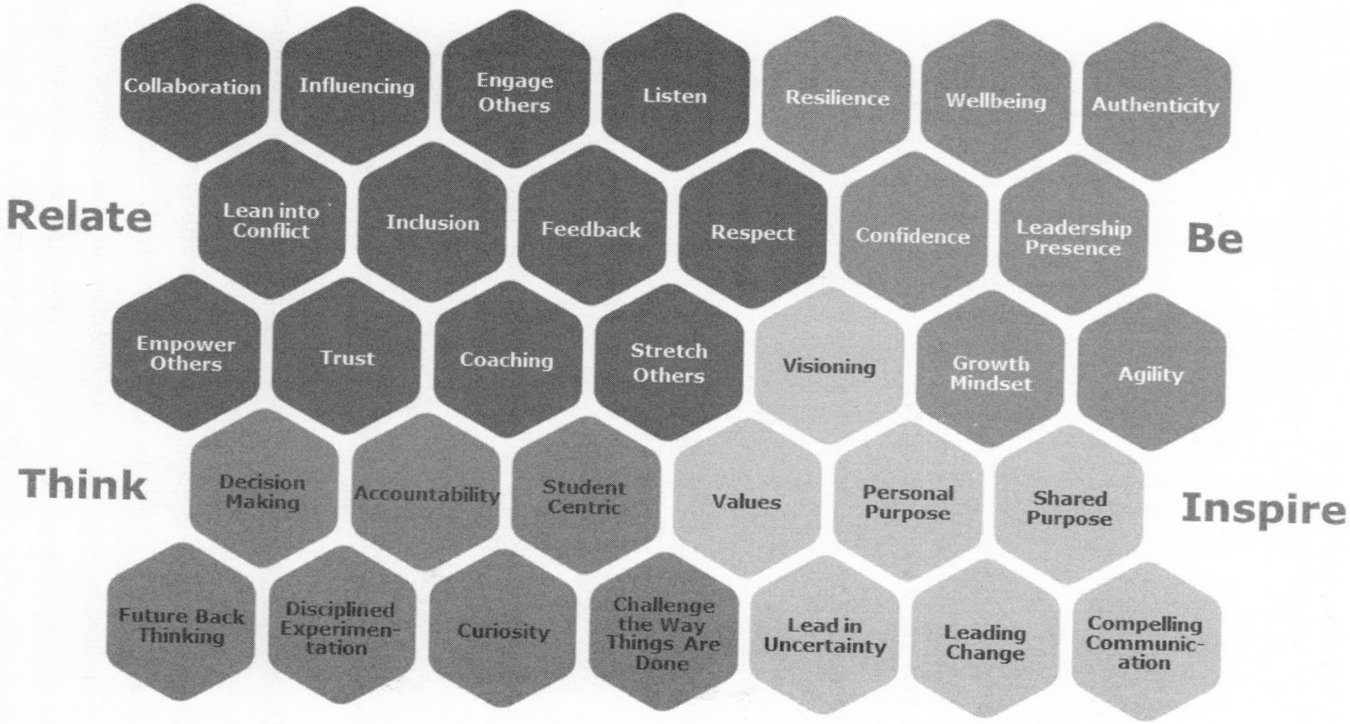

FIGURE 7.3
Top School Leadership Mindsets Featuring in Coaching Objectives

	BTS Spark North America	BTS Spark UK	BTS Spark Australia	BTS Spark All Regions
Leadership Mindset Shift	% objectives including this shift	% objectives including this shift	% objectives including this shift	% objectives including this shift
Feedback: It's something we both want.	19%	30%	20%	22%
Stretch Others: I develop and enable others.	12%	23%	20%	19%
Confidence: I act even when I'm afraid.	21%	13%	20%	19%
Engage Others: I can step into others' shoes.	13%	14%	19%	17%
Coaching: I guide from the side.	8%	10%	18%	15%
Resilience: I can choose my response.	6%	20%	10%	11%
Lean into Conflict: Difficult conversations lead to trust.	9%	11%	7%	8%
Accountability: I focus on what's important to deliver results.	4%	4%	10%	8%
Listen: I'm here with you.	9%	4%	9%	8%

Note: Each coaching objective was analyzed to identify two related leadership mindsets.

It's one thing to identify a mindset that is holding you back and a shift you'd like to make. Your intentions may be noble, but we know it's another thing entirely to actually make that shift and embrace an entirely new worldview. Has anyone ever told you that you *just* need to change your mindset? If they did, you probably found the advice deeply unhelpful, however well intentioned. Change is difficult.

With that in mind, let's explore a few fundamental strategies that support mindset shifts. Philosopher Ken Wilber (2000) offers a helpful tool to describe the process of internal transformation. His 3-2-1 process is simple to remember, composed of three successive stages:

3: You are blind to the new worldview.
2: You can see the new worldview.
1: You embrace the new worldview.

The insight that this process gives is the need to transition from the old mindset to the new mindset. Wilber emphasizes that, before you can embrace a new worldview or mindset, you need to take the time (in stage 2) to explore its many facets, even noticing previously disowned traits or shadows of your leadership. You can't just jump right in!

Our own model identifies four stages to making a sustained shift in leadership mindsets in order to grow and develop your leadership practice over the long term (Figure 7.4).

FIGURE 7.4
Four-Step Model to Support a Sustained Mindset Shift

Without professional and personalized support, you may find it difficult to make a true mindset shift. If you are serious about shifting mindsets—your own or others—and are unable to invest in coaching support, we recommend you dip into *The Four Greatest Coaching Conversations* (Connor & Hirani, 2019), which offers a how-to guide for shifting mindsets as well as more general guidance on the psychology behind mindsets. For now, we will share their summary of what stops people from changing. They identify four barriers:

1. **Don't forget the culture.** Our organizations have mindsets, too, that are embedded in their culture, and it's difficult to go against the grain.

2. **Old behaviors die hard.** Trying to change an old pattern requires conscious effort, experimentation, and dedicated learning.
3. **We're attached to a subpersonality.** We do not want to truly let go of our old identity, even when we know it's not serving us.
4. **We have the wrong attitude toward learning.** We fear risk-taking and failure and operate from a fixed mindset rather than a growth mindset.

If embracing new mindsets is important to leadership effectiveness but hard to achieve on your own, then how can professional development better support you?

Supporting Mindset Shifts with Professional Development

Most professional development for school leaders is organized by school systems, which vary considerably in their readiness to recognize the role that mindsets play in influencing leadership practice. The concept of mindsets may be conflated with soft skills, an area that has been demoted by many school systems in favor of instructional leadership approaches. In the last few years, though, some school systems have started to name several mindsets or dispositions they expect school leaders to embrace and model. A few have even introduced some form of soft skills assessment into their principal accreditation process. Very few of the school systems that have taken these steps, however, have taken the next step and provided professional development that specifically helps leaders embrace the mindsets they have identified as critical.

Given the difficulties in securing a strong, healthy pipeline of school leaders and encouraging sufficient applicants for principal vacancies, school systems don't have the luxury of writing off those who may not model all of their priority school leadership mindsets at the outset. Instead, they need to reconfigure traditional professional development offerings and invest in approaches that help school leaders make changes in their leadership practice by shifting the mindsets that may be holding them back from achieving their full potential.

We know that shifting mindsets takes time, dedication, and professional support. Professional development that is most effective in shifting mindsets involves a very different model than the traditional large-scale one-off conferences of the past. Instead, it requires small-group and personalized one-on-one support over time. This enables school leaders to become more aware of their mindsets, experiment with new approaches, reflect, and learn in a continuous action learning cycle. Supporting others as they shift their mindsets is skilled work, which requires specific training in transformational approaches and years of experience to achieve true mastery. This is the domain of professional leadership coaches, rather than the retired school principals who so often lead professional development with the aim of sharing their wisdom with the next generation of school leaders.

The MESSY leadership model reveals some of the mindsets that school leaders most need to embrace as they lead their school communities through times of uncertainty. It provokes school systems to rethink the way they identify talent and then develop, reward, and nurture leaders. Business-as-usual leadership development will not work. Reverting to past training, performance management, and processes will produce past results. To maintain and nurture extraordinary leadership, school systems need to take a different approach. They need to help their leaders let go of old beliefs that underpin unhelpful practices. Mindsets such as "I need to be in control," "I am responsible," "I need to be stoic," and "I need to focus on a clear plan for the future" are likely to be counterproductive.

Unfortunately, most school systems reinforce these beliefs in countless ways, from a focus on process (implying "I need to be in control") to school improvement planning processes (with the implicit belief that "I need to focus on a clear plan for the future"). New mindsets such as "It is OK to be human," "We are constantly learning more about the future," "Change is something I learn from," and "I trust myself to see what is needed" carry implications for principals, department heads, and superintendents and for how we run our schools. This does not mean abandoning the processes, structures, and tools that make school systems effective, but it does mean leveraging them in a much more dynamic way.

Acknowledging mindsets as a critical component of professional development for leaders is crucial to our ability to transform school communities. If we are going to transform systems, then we must transform ourselves—and that work begins with mindset.

> *"I've realized that I need to make a mindset shift. Instead of being stuck and frustrated with the slow pace of change, I see now that I can make change happen, and it starts with me."*

8

Coaching Others in MESSY Leadership

So far, we've explored the characteristics of MESSY leadership and explained how a MESSY leadership approach will help you face the challenges of leading schools in today's uncertain climate. We've also shown how you need to pay attention to shifting your mindset if you want to make a sustained shift in your leadership practice and behaviors.

As a leader, you can strengthen and improve your own leadership capabilities, but you are probably not the only leader in your school. You can, however, be the spark that helps individuals on your team reflect on and grow their own capabilities. So how do you go about helping colleagues adopt these more collaborative, emotionally intelligent, future-focused, and adaptive leadership approaches?

One easy way to get started is simply by sharing parts of your own leadership journey with your team. When leaders show vulnerability, it humanizes them, makes them more relatable, and contributes to the creation of a learning culture. If your team sees that you are reflective and working to improve your own leadership, it can serve as both inspiration and permission for them to embrace their own vulnerabilities.

You could also use the MESSY leadership monitor (Appendix A) to help your team determine their strengths and potential areas of growth. If they are willing to share this information with you, then you'll have valuable insight into where you should start with your team. Alternatively, you could simply ask each team member which of the areas they feel strongest in and which they feel most drawn to in order to develop and grow their own leadership. You could then conduct a book study or lead a team read of a particular chapter and select one or more of the go-do actions to start integrating the MESSY tools into your everyday practice. For a printable toolkit of MESSY leadership resources to share with your team, go to https://btsspark.org/messyleadership.

Want to go a step further and provide individualized support to your colleagues? Good news! Many of the tools and strategies you've been learning throughout this book can help you start coaching your colleagues to get MESSY:

- See Hear Speak (Chapter 2) gives you a structured process for building relational trust with a colleague so they can feel safe and open to trying new approaches and learning with you.
- Mindtraps (Chapter 6) may be holding your colleague back from changing their leadership practice. You can explore the different mindtraps and use the ETC process to help your colleague find a way forward.
- The MBIR framework (Chapter 7) offers a structure for setting a development goal with your colleague.

As you start working with colleagues in a coachlike way, it will quickly become obvious that everyone needs a different approach. Professional coaches have a repertoire of strategies for meeting the wide-ranging needs of the different people they coach. In the rest of this chapter, we'll share a simple model to help you differentiate your coaching to meet individuals where they are.

Building Capability by Coaching Others

The concept of "leader as coach" can be helpful when thinking about leadership styles that fully develop the capabilities of others. This requires leaders to embrace a coaching skillset that may or may not have been a part of their formal leadership training, and it may call on a very different style of leadership than they are accustomed to.

> *"I tend to react to issues quickly. I need to shift from thinking 'This is proof I am a good leader as I am getting things done' to 'It's really important that my team members grow and develop.'"*

As a school leader, you probably find yourself coaching others all the time, whether you realize it or not. New teachers come to you asking for advice, parents come to you with problems, colleagues ask for feedback... the coaching moments in daily school life are endless. Even though you may not consider yourself to be a coach, you most likely have a natural coaching style, whether you are aware of it or not. The "four faces of coaching" describe four very different coaching styles, each with its own merits:

- **Challengers** are great at giving constructive feedback and encouraging others to break the mold and explore new ways of working. They are leaders who challenge people's thinking and help them see possibilities beyond the status quo. Challengers hold up a mirror and help people identify their own blind spots, positive or negative.
- **Explorers** provide emotional support and are great listeners. They are good at getting under the surface of an issue and to the heart of what is wrong. By taking a step back, explorers help people view old problems in new ways, enabling them to find their own solution to an issue.

- **Experts** share their experience and knowledge, offering clear guidance and actionable steps to help people tackle a difficult challenge. They explain things in a clear and compelling way. Experts are respected and regularly sought out for advice.
- **Supporters** build confidence within those around them. They encourage people to believe in themselves and take on new challenges. Supporters easily see the best in people, spot their potential, and give praise. They intentionally give stretch tasks to encourage people to grow their capabilities.

Which is your most natural coaching style? Which do you gravitate toward when working with others? It's likely that one of the four faces stands out as a strength, and one doesn't resonate with your natural style as much. This presents a challenge for most school leaders and affects their ability to be truly responsive and flexible to the needs of others. As a busy school leader, it is easy to stay in—and coach others from—your own leadership comfort zone. However, the most effective leaders know when to flex their style and how to shift their coaching behaviors to get the best out of their team.

Do you remember Olivia from Chapter 2? As Olivia learned to reflect on her coaching style, she realized that she had been relying on the expert coaching face, providing solutions to issues based on her previous experiences. However, what most people on her team needed was either a challenger (giving clear, constructive feedback) or a supporter (empowering them to solve problems themselves). Olivia experimented with the different faces of coaching and experienced greater success when she adjusted her approach to meet the specific needs of each person on her team.

If you'd like to review your natural coaching style, spend a few minutes completing the Four Faces of Coaching Questionnaire in Appendix C. It's important to note that the four faces offer different styles—*not personalities*—and everyone can learn new styles. The most adept leaders are those who can adjust their style to meet the needs of the situation, and they are open to adjustments and willing to seek improvement.

Take a moment to reflect on yourself as a coach. What types of coaching conversations are you comfortable leading? What types of conversations do you shy away from? Now think about the people in your school and the different types of coaching conversations they need to perform at their best. Who needs a coaching conversation? This doesn't always have an easy answer since many schools operate within the "culture of nice"—a culture that accepts everyone as is but doesn't welcome improvement conversations at the individual level.

As you reflect, you'll likely notice that you overuse some coaching faces and underuse (or even completely neglect) others. However, to meet the diverse coaching needs of people on your team, you should be deploying all four faces of coaching. The most effective coaching happens when coaches can blend their own strengths with a style that best fits the person on the receiving end.

Flexing Your Style with the Four Faces of Coaching

With the four faces model as the backdrop, there are two additional concepts that will help you more effectively coach and empower your team: skill/will and push/pull. To really appreciate how these concepts can be utilized in a coaching context, take a moment to identify someone on your team you would really like to empower—someone you would like to coach so they can achieve their best and maximize their impact.

With a member of your team in mind, think about their current performance and capabilities. What is getting in their way of leveling up their performance: skill or will? A skill growth area is one that aims to improve a person's understanding of a subject, their ability to use a strategy, or their capacity to do a job. Skill growth areas often happen when someone is new to a role or when there are new skills expected of them. By contrast, a will growth area is one that aims to shift a person's underlying attitude, such as their confidence, resilience, or motivation. For example, will growth areas may show up with more experienced people who know how to do things but may have attitudinal issues that influence their effectiveness at work. If you can clarify whether the person you are coaching is facing a skill issue or a will issue, it will help you understand what kind of coaching support they will most benefit from.

> *"I've had the realization that not everyone is like me, and I need to flex my leadership style to suit the needs of other people."*

Now that you know whether the team member is struggling with a skill issue or a will issue, you can identify the correct approach to take: push or pull. Push strategies are where the leader gives guidance, shares ideas, and convinces the other person to try new ideas. These strategies are most effective when the individual needs to be challenged. By contrast, pull strategies are where the leader asks the individual for their improvement ideas. In this case, learning is pulled along by the desires or goals of the individual. This is important when the individual has the knowledge in their head and just needs to be asked the right questions.

Once you've identified whether the person you are coaching is facing a skill or a will issue, and whether they would benefit from a push or a pull coaching strategy, the Four Faces of Coaching Matrix (Figure 8.1) shows which coaching face you need to adopt in your coaching conversation.

Olivia, for example, realized that she needed to work very differently with the many teachers in her school who were already open to changing their practice: the early adopters. These teachers faced a skill issue and needed Olivia to adopt a pull coaching strategy (i.e., they needed a supporter). With a little upskilling early on, Olivia soon found that they responded well to being asked to trial a new strategy and run with it.

As a school leader, it is nearly impossible to meet the needs of everyone in your school community. However, the four faces of coaching will help you meet the coaching needs of your immediate team members: your teachers and staff. Like skipping a rock in calm water, coaching individuals for growth creates

FIGURE 8.1
Four Faces of Coaching Matrix

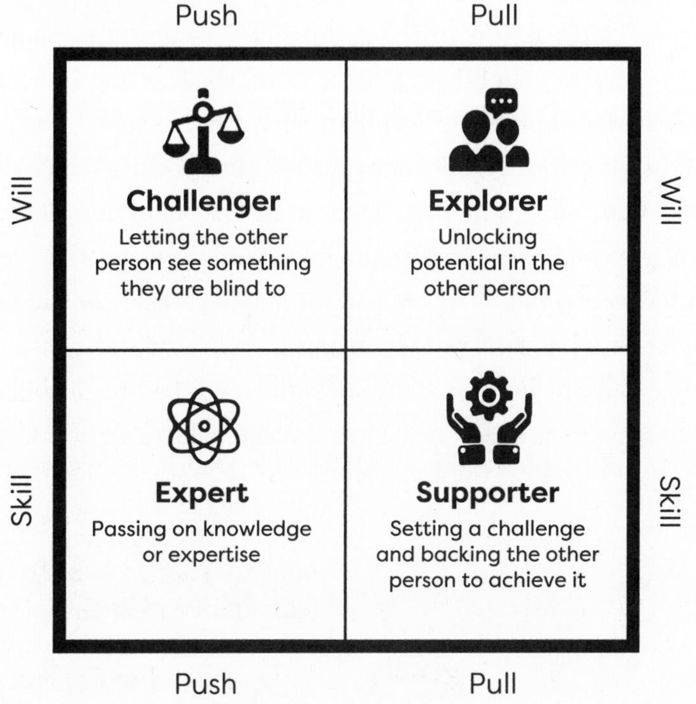

ripples that cascade outward and positively change the culture of your school for a long time.

Empowering Others

In education, there is much talk about empowerment. We talk about empowering our students and teachers, but what do we really mean by that? *Empowerment* has become another cliché word used when talking about improving education. It's easy to say, but it's much harder to put into practice. Have you ever had the experience of trying your best to empower others only to end up frustrated that they don't seem to take the initiative to get things done? If so, you are not alone. In fact, this comes up frequently in our coaching conversations with school leaders. The million-dollar question seems to be "How do I empower my team to solve their own problems?"

To empower others, you'll need to further develop the supporter face of coaching. Supporters help others believe in themselves and in what they are capable of accomplishing. Most people underestimate their own capabilities and are overly self-critical. When individuals receive positive feedback on things they do well, it encourages them to do more of those behaviors. Supporters are also particularly good at putting people in situations where they are stretched to unearth their potential. They are good at helping others own and solve their own problems, providing the right level of support so the stretch isn't too great. Finally, supporters are willing to trust individuals on their team with significant tasks, allowing them the space to make mistakes and learn while doing it.

When team members show a lack of engagement, it may have more to do with you the leader than with the individuals on the team. Take a moment to reflect on what is holding you back from empowering your team. There may be mindsets or mindtraps that are getting in your way.

A school principal shared this insight they had in coaching: "So often as leaders we believe that we are doing the best for everyone by taking on everything, but true leadership involves including others in the process." People disengage when they aren't challenged or don't feel like they are having an impact. To empower your team, try giving them more responsibility, thereby creating a cycle of trust. When you delegate important work, you communicate to your team that you believe in them and are creating an opportunity for them to step into a capability gap. Empowerment will increase when every individual on your team has responsibility, autonomy, and accountability. By listening, using your supporter coaching face, and creating stretch opportunities, you are not only empowering your team but also giving individuals a chance to shine.

> *"If I break the nice and be nicer cycle, I can empower teachers. When next that person comes to seek permission for something they could themselves decide, I will explain that I trust them with the decision-making and then discuss different ways of our working together."*

Spotting Coaching Moments

It's common to feel paralyzed into inaction when you hear encouragements to coach and empower your team. It can feel like an impossible task to add coaching to your already very long to-do list. If that's you, then read on!

Keep in mind that nobody is asking you to become a professional coach overnight. Coaching is a profession, and most of the coaches we employ at BTS Spark have been full-time professional coaches for over a decade. They have the expertise to support leaders as they make critical mindset shifts. On the other hand, what we are encouraging you to do is lead in a coachlike way. Slow down, take the time to listen and understand others' needs, flex your style to meet those needs, and identify opportunities for others to stretch themselves (rather than "rescuing" them by fixing their problems).

There's a myth that all coaching conversations need to be lengthy, structured, and formal—and take place during a dedicated time set aside for coaching. The "leader as coach" approach challenges this by advocating coaching on the go. You can have a huge impact by asking just a single powerful question or by integrating one of the MESSY tools into a casual conversation. The trick is to spot a coaching moment and then seize it. Try it, and you could surprise yourself!

9

Developing Your MESSY Leadership Capabilities

Sarah, a hardworking department head, found herself in survival mode. She spent each day responding to issues at school, solving problems, and checking things off her never-ending to-do list, and she was left feeling exhausted and a little uninspired by it all. It was hard to reconnect with the passion she felt earlier in her career. The more work there was to do, the more Sarah felt the need to hunker down and take on more of the tasks herself. In many ways, this felt like the right thing to do. It felt more efficient—like she was lightening the workload for her team, knowing they already had full plates. However, working in task-orientated isolation started to take a toll on Sarah and her ability to lead. As hard as she was working, she wasn't having the impact she desired, nor did she have a sense of fulfillment from her job.

If she wanted to get different results, Sarah would need to shift her leadership practices, but she didn't know where to begin. Sound familiar? Unfortunately, this experience is very common among school leaders. Too many school leaders feel unfulfilled and exhausted in their roles and find themselves questioning whether they should continue. It can feel daunting to unpack the challenges and get the support you need and deserve. MESSY leadership is an antidote to many of the challenges experienced by school leaders. There is a better, more fulfilling way to lead your school—and it can be learned. No matter how many years of experience you have, you can choose to shift your mindset and lean into new ways of leading.

We have established how messy school leadership really is. It's filled with complex problems, ambiguous and conflicting demands, and competing priorities. Becoming a MESSY leader is about embracing that messiness and mastering the leadership skills and mindsets needed to lead confidently, despite the uncertainty. To make these shifts successfully, you need to embrace a strong sense of self and purpose to build trust and navigate complexity. Our intention with this book was to provide a resource filled with insights, knowledge, and practical tools you can implement in your day-to-day work.

We also know firsthand the challenge of implementation. You may have found this book aspirational yet still find yourself overwhelmed without knowing exactly where and how to begin. Maybe you have already begun experimenting with strategies to shift your mindset but are finding it hard to sustain, given the busyness of your everyday life. This final chapter will provide guidance and inspiration for how you might build your own MESSY leadership capabilities and the capabilities of your team.

Olivia, the principal in Chapter 2, was strong in her convictions as a leader and had a vision for the future of her school. The problem was that her vision wasn't a shared one. She realized she was setting the direction and doing much of the work, but no one was following her. Her first step was to learn how to include others and collaborate on a vision. Olivia reflected, "I didn't realize how extremely stressed I was carrying so much of the workload on my own. I've had to learn how to really collaborate with my team and in the process have found my stress level is much lower."

John, the elementary school principal in Chapter 3, realized many of his relationships were superficial and that he was avoiding having the hard conversations.

His starting point was to work on shifting his mindset around feedback. He worked to reframe feedback as a gift and started using feedback protocols. John reflected on this work, sharing, "I'm learning how to step into conflict more confidently and feel more confident having difficult conversations."

Stephen, the administrator in Chapter 5, was really struggling to find the best way to make an impact with so many policies and mandates. His starting point was to identify what was in his control and sphere of influence, despite the top-down directives. Stephen reflected, "Previously, I would shy away from sharing policy information as it always seems to change, but now I feel confident providing interim information as a heads-up, knowing my team will appreciate it's a moment in time and may change without notice. If the policy changes, it's not a reflection on me or my leadership. I am more trusting of my team and their strengths. They require updates to feel part of the whole system and not just a passive audience."

Tony, the principal of a large high school in Chapter 6, was having a confidence issue despite many years of experience. His starting point was to own who he was as a leader and give up the notion that he had to be all things to all people. He embraced his strengths and learned to draw on his sources of authentic confidence, taking stock of all he had accomplished and the experiences he brought to the role. When feeling unsure, he would revisit this list. Tony shared, "As simple as it sounds, I'm learning the importance of checking my own self-talk and adding *yet* to some sentences to enable me to give myself time to learn and grow. The same as we would for our students. I'm learning to be kind to myself."

Each of these leaders had their own unique pain points and, as a result, took different first steps to shift their mindset and leadership practice. Likewise, you are unique, so your growth journey will also be unique. The goal here is not to feel overwhelmed but to identify your pain point and the first step you can take to address it. Too often, leaders want to take it all on at once, working to improve every aspect of their leadership. That intent may be noble, but it just isn't realistic or sustainable. Leaders who take on too many self-improvement initiatives at once end up feeling overwhelmed and defeated. From our work with more than

20,000 school leaders, we know that the best path forward is to identify, select, and prioritize one growth area at a time and then work with a simple strategy or two to improve. As one of our coaches reminds us, "It doesn't need to be hard to be valuable. Start with simple, then acknowledge and celebrate small successes as you grow."

Writing a Letter from the Future

To stay inspired, you must constantly revisit your growth and rededicate yourself to the journey. Without this, the day-to-day distractions of work can obscure your personal vision and stop your forward momentum. If starting from a pain point feels too challenging, try focusing on your future leadership self by taking half an hour to write yourself a letter from the future.

Imagine it is many years from now and you have achieved your most meaningful life goals both personally and professionally. You are reflecting on the journey. From this perspective, write a letter to yourself today. Pick a time you can envision but that is far enough away that you can still dream, imagine, and be open to the many possibilities out there waiting for you. Most people find it easiest to pick a particular date that means something to them, such as 10 years from now or a special milestone (e.g., retirement, anniversary). As you reflect and write the letter, ask yourself the following questions:

- What was the experience like?
- What are you remembered for?
- What did you stand for?
- What will people say about the way you went about your leadership?
- What is your legacy?
- What are the biggest changes you were able to bring about?
- What obstacles and hurdles did you overcome?

You get to create this experience, so make it great. Be totally creative! Anything is possible. Go to a quiet place where you will not be disturbed so you can enjoy the creative process in solitude. Taking time to reflect on what you can accomplish and what is important to you may help you identify the areas of your leadership you want to work on or improve the most. Once written, share your letter with a colleague (to keep you accountable) and then tuck it away somewhere you'll remember to revisit it from time to time.

Finding Your Support Network

Leadership can be inherently isolating, especially when you are trying to improve your leadership capabilities. How do you hold yourself accountable? Who do you trust to have honest conversations about the times you aren't showing up as your best self? With whom do you want to share the highs and lows of your leadership journey? These aren't always easy conversations to have, but they are necessary and will help you achieve the leadership shifts you want to see. It's worth taking a few minutes to jot down who's in your corner and who you can rely on in your support network. It may be more than one person, and you may identify different people for different types of support. The goal is to identify one or more people with whom you can be vulnerable, take off your mask, and just be yourself.

We recently surveyed principals and asked, "Who do you tend to go to for support with leadership challenges?" Their responses (they could select more than one source of support) highlight a number of important sources:

- Peer/principal colleague: 73%
- Trusted colleague: 55%
- Director/superintendent: 41%
- Senior leadership team: 36%
- Family member or friend: 18%
- Mentor: 9%
- Professional coach: 5%

Sadly, 5 percent of principals felt that they had *nobody* to turn to for support with their leadership challenges. What questions does this list raise for you? Are there people in your network you could reach out to who might provide you with the opportunity to debrief, offload, or find a new sense of direction? The point here is that you don't have to navigate the challenges of leadership alone and are much more likely to achieve all your goals if you have the backing of a carefully selected support network.

Shifting Your Mindset Using MESSY Tools and Strategies

Throughout this book, we have shared leadership models, tools, and strategies intended to help you develop your leadership capabilities. For ease of reference, Figure 9.1 summarizes each of these, including a brief description, the purpose of the tool, and a helpful insight from a school leader who had success with it. The goal here is to provide a handy reference you can use when you or your team are facing a new challenge and need a new approach.

Global business leaders such as Bill Gates, Sheryl Sandberg, and Eric Schmidt have publicly spoken about the impact of coaching on their leadership. Schmidt highlights the value of coaching in *Trillion Dollar Coach* (Schmidt et al., 2019), where he shares insights and lessons learned from his experience working with Bill Campbell, a renowned executive coach, and the impact it had on his leadership journey and the success of Google. At BTS Spark, we believe leadership coaching is not just a luxury that should be reserved for chief executives. We see coaching as a necessary support that all school leaders should have access to for long-term growth, sustainability, and job fulfillment. However, to date, leadership coaching has been slow to gain traction in many education systems.

Instructional coaching has gained popularity in schools because it is effective at improving teaching practices and student outcomes. Research studies (e.g., Goldhaber et al., 2020; Matthews, 2019) and anecdotal evidence suggest that instructional coaching can improve teaching practices, enhance teacher effectiveness, and ultimately lead to improved student outcomes. Instructional coaching is more effective than the traditional professional development workshop model because coaching is typically personalized and integrated into teachers' day-to-day activities. Indeed, Kraft, Blazar, and Hogan (2018) created a meta-analysis of 60 instructional coaching evaluations and found that instructional coaching had a strong positive effect on instructional practice (0.49 standard deviations). Helping teachers improve their instructional practice has been a high priority for schools for many years and students are reaping the benefits.

FIGURE 9.1

A Summary of MESSY Tools and Strategies

Tool	Description and Purpose	Insight
	Chapter 1	
Me Us It	Getting the balance right between yourself (me), your relationships (us), and the work to be done (it).	"My coach had me draw my own version of Me Us It with each circle representing how I spent my time and writing the types of things I did inside the circles. I had a sense that I was out of balance, but this made it crystal clear."
	Chapter 2: Meaning Making	
Rubber Band	Creating a vision; helping to ground you in your current reality, identify your vision, and determine if there is enough stretch or tension in the "rubber band" between your reality and vision.	"This tool helped me see that we didn't have enough tension between our current reality and vision. We need to think bigger!"
See Hear Speak	Building rapport and grounding all relationships in empathy; reminding you to make sure that people feel seen and heard before you speak to them. The order is important: see, hear, and then speak.	"These three simple steps are so effective. This would be great as a sign in my office as a visual reminder to stop talking or monopolizing conversations."
The Presence Triangle	Achieving a breakthrough in a challenging relationship by stepping into another person's shoes and using your new insight to shift the relationship dynamic. The Presence Triangle focuses on self, others, and conditions to increase trust, connection, and safety.	"I used the Presence Triangle when a situation arose with a teacher who sent school leadership a difficult email. I explained the tool to my co-head, and we practiced stepping into the teacher's shoes. This allowed us to respond in a more measured and constructive way to her email."

(continued)

FIGURE 9.1 *(Continued)*

Tool	Description and Purpose	Insight
Chapter 3: Emotional Connection		
Iceberg Model of Relationships	Going deeper to build trust by appreciating the three different dimensions of relationships: social, business, and trust.	"This model helped me realize how many of my relationships fall in the social realm."
Feedback Traps	Challenging yourself to recognize the different traps that may be holding you back from giving feedback. Feedback traps include avoidance, abdication, pleasing, skill, and fear.	"I am guilty of all these traps. Yikes! Now that I am aware of them, I want to challenge myself to no longer fall into them."
WWW-EBI Framework	Giving everyday feedback on the job with a simple but effective tool to give frequent feedback. WWW = *What went well?* EBI = *Even better if . . .*	"I like the simplicity of the framework and am using it as an exit ticket from staff meetings as a less threatening way to ask about our leadership."
A FIRM Framework	Preparing for a potentially difficult feedback conversation where you need to address an unhelpful pattern of behavior. A FIRM includes agenda, facts, impact, request, and mutuality.	"This model is excellent. I have applied this in several situations, and it makes difficult conversations easier, but I can't stress enough how important the preparation for the conversation is."
Chapter 4: Sensing the Future		
Rivers of Thinking	Making you more aware of the mental pathways that influence how you interpret information, what you see in the world around you, and how you respond.	"Doing small things differently in my daily routine, like driving a different route to school or changing up the order of how I start work, is helping me see that although my rivers of thinking are strong, it is possible and refreshing to change them."
Breakthrough Thinking Cycle	A model to help tackle entrenched school improvement issues in a systematic way. The Breakthrough Thinking Cycle consists of (1) looking up, (2) looking out, (3) looking down, (4) looking forward, and (5) looking in.	"This model felt very overwhelming to me until I just started focusing on one stage at a time. I like the reminder of where to look at each stage."

Tool	Description and Purpose	Insight
Asking Three *Whys*	Uncovering one or two root causes behind the issue you are tackling by digging down below the surface and asking *why* three times.	"Such a simple strategy and yet one that very quickly helped my team uncover how inconsistent practices from teacher to teacher were affecting student behavior."
Bop It	Prompts to help come up with new ideas by playing with the rules that bind your current challenge. Prompts include stretch it, shrink it, twist it, turn it, whack it, smack it, spend it, and save it.	"While fun, this was way harder than I could have anticipated. I realized how constrained my thinking has become over the years. Retraining yourself to be more playful in your thinking leads to bigger and better ideas."
Chapter 5: Seizing Momentum		
Three *Ps*	Raising your awareness of what is supporting or hindering your personal effectiveness by focusing on proactivity, procrastination, and prioritization.	"I don't think I'll ever think of procrastination the same way. I now challenge myself to identify why I'm procrastinating getting something done; it's rarely about the time it takes."
Eisenhower Prioritization Matrix	Prioritizing how you spend your time by rating your tasks on their urgency and importance in order to determine whether to do, decide to schedule, delegate, or delete them.	"I used to act fast and knock things on the head, but now the prioritization matrix helps me see I was spending time quickly working through things that didn't really matter."
Push and Pull of Change	The push (the positive changes you want to make) and the pull (the chains that hold you back) of change help you gain clarity on the forces at play that could support or hinder you in achieving the positive change you want to make.	"The simple visual is a great reminder for me. I get so focused on the changes we want to make that I forget there are chains holding people back."
Chapter 6: Your Presence		
In the Box and Out of the Box	Raising awareness of your current state of resourcefulness and what triggers can influence your leadership effectiveness. In the box = not showing up as your best self; out of the box = showing up as your best self, full of optimism and creativity.	"I created a list of things that help me get out of the box (take a walk, stretch, call a friend, put on music in my office) and learned that by doing these more often, I am less likely to be triggered as easily."

(continued)

FIGURE 9.1 *(Continued)*

Tool	Description and Purpose	Insight
Mindtraps	Recognizing the unproductive inner thoughts or self-talk that distort the reality of a situation, causing you to jump to conclusions or assume the worst. Mindtraps can hugely affect your leadership effectiveness.	"Becoming aware of these mindtraps helped me feel less alone; I now see how all leaders struggle. Armed with this knowledge, I am more conscious of my mindset and can choose to avoid the negative self-talk."
Emotion Truth Choice	A three-step process to help self-regulate or find a more balanced perspective and a resourceful state, particularly at times of stress, by breaking free from your exaggerated pessimistic and judging thoughts so you can make a conscious choice about how to react.	"I am now so much more aware of my inner pessimist and judge voices. Separating my emotion from the truth has been a real growth area for me as a leader."
	Chapter 7	
MBIR Framework	Getting clarity on the shift you want to see in your leadership by focusing on the shift at four levels. MBIR stands for mindset, behavior, impact, and results.	"Utilizing the MBIR framework helped me see that, previously, I focused on trying to shift or change my behaviors, but the changes weren't sustainable as I hadn't shifted my mindset."
	Chapter 8	
Four Faces of Coaching	Four Faces of Coaching include challenger, explorer, expert, and supporter. This model outlines the different styles you can use to coach and empower others, helping you also identify if people are struggling with a skill or will issue.	"I intentionally used the coaching style of the supporter with a new staff member who feels a little out of their depth with their new role. I just need to build their confidence as they have the skills."

Unfortunately, there hasn't been a similar sustained focus on helping school leaders improve their leadership capabilities, even though the impact a highly effective principal makes is profound. A recent study commissioned by the Wallace Foundation found the quality of school leadership has a massive impact on students and their achievement. Just by replacing a "below average" school principal with an "above average" principal, the average student gains an additional three months of learning in math and reading (Grissom et al., 2021). Imagine the difference it could make for students if, instead of replacing ineffective principals, we invested heavily in leadership development and grew the great leaders every school deserves.

Leadership coaching has the power to enhance effectiveness, develop self-awareness, and drive personal and professional growth. It provides support, feedback, and guidance to help leaders gain insights, overcome challenges, and leverage their strengths. It leads to improved communication, decision-making, problem-solving, and interpersonal skills, ultimately enabling leaders to achieve their full potential, inspire and motivate others, and drive organizational success.

Research that points to the efficacy of leadership coaching is important, but we find that direct feedback from school and district leaders is the most compelling evidence of the potential impact coaching has on leaders. We will share an example.

Retired superintendent Jordan Tinney shared why coaching became his preferred method for his own professional development:

> Rather than travelling to conferences, watching presentations or speakers, I found someone to coach me, to hold my feet to the fire about my own strategic plans, initiatives, and goals. To me, the change was transformational. It wasn't transformational because I learned new things; it was transformational because I had someone at my side, a confidante, to hold me personally accountable for the work I committed to do. (Tinney & O'Brien, 2020, para. 5)

Based on his personal experience with coaching, Tinney created an opportunity for all school leaders in his large, urban school district to access leadership coaching. The first offering was a voluntary summer coaching program for school leaders that focused on resilience and well-being. BTS Spark designed a custom blended coaching journey including both one-on-one and small-group coaching to help leaders process higher levels of stress and become more skilled at leading despite uncertainty. The Surviving to Thriving coaching program was offered to all school leaders but, given the timing over the summer break, Tinney expected no more than a dozen leaders to opt into the program.

Imagine our collective surprise and delight when 85 school leaders signed up to be a part of this summer coaching journey. Engagement was high, and feedback from the coaching journey—both formal and anecdotal—was extremely strong. Participants were surveyed both before and after the program, and their responses consistently showed positive experiences. As a result of the program, school leaders reported being more able to manage their state, stay resilient, achieve a work-life balance, deal with energy-sapping relationships, tackle difficult conversations, and go into the new school year with a clear vision (see Figure 9.2). All those surveyed said that they would recommend coaching to colleagues. As you can see, coaching made a significant difference for these leaders.

We believe leadership coaching is significantly underutilized in education likely because there are many misconceptions about coaching. People sometimes think that great coaching can't be scaled, that it can have personal impact

FIGURE 9.2
The Impact of Coaching on School Leaders

	Before	After
I have strategies to stay resilient and effective in stressful situations.	64%	100%
I am able to create balance in my life.	44%	90%
I have a clear vision for the new school year.	43%	100%
I feel that I have the tools to manage energy-sapping relationships.	30%	100%
I feel confident having difficult conversations.	39%	90%

Source: From "Professional Well-Being Through Coaching," by J. Tinney and T. O'Brien, 2020. https://www.edcan.ca/articles/professional-well-being-through-coaching. Copyright 2020 by The EdCan Network. Reprinted with permission.

but not lead to systemic improvement, or that it's only affordable for very senior leaders. Having coached 20,000 leaders, our point of view is very different. We believe coaching can be consistently scalable, is the best tool to support change and transformation, creates the most powerful insight data you can get, and can be extremely affordable. Coaching, whether instructional or transformational, helps people achieve change faster.

Anytime you learn something new, you progress through four psychological stages of conscious competence (Curtiss & Warren, 1973). These stages can be applied to anything, but let's apply them to a principal leading a school:

1. **Unconscious Incompetence:** In this stage, a principal may aspire to lead effectively but may not fully understand the complexities and responsibilities involved in the role. They may not be aware of all the complexities involved in managing staff, implementing educational policies, overseeing curriculum development, and fostering a positive school culture. They may underestimate the challenges and intricacies of the position.
2. **Conscious Incompetence:** In this stage, a principal may become aware of their lack of competence and knowledge in school leadership. They realize the importance of skills such as strategic planning, instructional leadership, budget management, community engagement, and staff development. They may seek professional development opportunities, pursue advanced degrees, or engage in mentorship programs to gain the necessary knowledge and skills required for effective school leadership.
3. **Conscious Competence:** A principal in this stage has acquired the necessary knowledge and skills through their professional development and experience. They can apply leadership principles and strategies to their role. They can effectively manage the school's operations, collaborate with staff, make informed decisions, and create a positive and productive learning environment. However, they need to consciously think about and apply their skills in different situations, relying on their training and expertise to lead the school effectively.

4. **Unconscious Competence:** In this final stage, a principal has internalized their knowledge and skills to the point where effective leadership becomes second nature. They can effortlessly navigate complex situations, make decisions based on intuition and experience, and inspire and motivate their staff. They have a deep understanding of educational leadership and can adapt their leadership style to the needs of their school and community. Leading the school becomes a natural and ingrained part of who they are as educational leaders.

School leaders may find themselves moving back and forth between the stages as they encounter new challenges, refine their leadership skills, and strive to meet the changing demands of their role. Leadership coaching is the most effective tool to help leaders move through the stages and get to unconscious competence. As you reflect on your own leadership, what levels of competence have you experienced?

At the end of every coaching journey, we solicit feedback from leaders about their coaching experience. Here is a sampling of actual comments from leaders:

- "The mountains I had in my mind about my role have become hills."
- "I could see what I was doing but could not see a way out or through my challenges. I have a clear path forward now."
- "Coaching enabled me to answer some of the most challenging questions I ask myself."
- "The coaching was incredibly useful! I now have more clarity, many more perspectives, and numerous strategies to put in place. I feel far more confident to take action, and I know that I will be far more effective in the action that I take."
- "My mind has been blown! I can never look at things in the same way again. I can never go back to thinking, feeling, and acting in the same way I did before."
- "It is really valuable to have someone to talk things through with. I feel much calmer now, like 'Bring it on!'"

- "I can't believe how huge a shift has happened in one hour. I came to the call extremely stressed and worried and left with a spring in my step, feeling hope and enthusiasm."

Let's circle back to Sarah. Recall that she was feeling depleted and uninspired in her leadership. She was fortunate to get support through a series of coaching conversations and is now recommitted to her work as a school leader and finding fulfillment in her work. Sarah shared,

> My biggest learning is a huge gift. Through coaching, I now see I am enough. This is a huge shift for me. Before my coaching started, I was feeling lost. This feeling has now totally gone. My coach breaks down the process and reflects what she is seeing back to me. I feel totally empowered. I now recognize the tools I already have, and each coaching conversation gives me the confidence to tackle new challenges. Prior to the coaching, when I was 'in the box,' I would just accept it and stay there, not even aware that I had options. And I spent a lot of my time 'in the box.' Now I'm not only aware of this earlier, but I have tools to get out and find a new perspective. I'm enjoying growing as a leader every day."

Remember, becoming an effective MESSY leader is a continuous journey, so be patient, persistent, and kind to yourself in the process. Our schools need you and your leadership. For additional free resources (a printable toolkit and presentation slides) to support you and your colleagues on your journey to becoming MESSY leaders, visit https://btsspark.org/messyleadership.

Appendix A

MESSY Leadership Monitor

We have aggregated all the MESSY monitors from each chapter to create this comprehensive MESSY leadership monitor. Where would you rate yourself on these MESSY leadership behaviors? Take some time to reflect on your leadership and give yourself an honest baseline for your current leadership practices. If you are seriously committed to accelerating your leadership development, copy this monitor and invite a colleague to provide feedback, then discuss their responses together.

Meaning Making Behaviors	Never	Rarely	Sometimes	Frequently	Very Often
My work is driven by a clear sense of purpose.					
I am confident while co-creating a vision with others.					
When leading change, I listen to what others have to say and am open to shifting my own point of view.					

Meaning Making Behaviors	Never	Rarely	Sometimes	Frequently	Very Often
I demonstrate empathy by stepping into another person's shoes to try and feel what they are feeling.					
I can collaborate effectively in a team setting.					
I empower my team to take ownership and accountability.					
I am comfortable letting go and trusting others.					

Emotional Connection Behaviors	Never	Rarely	Sometimes	Frequently	Very Often
I have deep, trusting relationships with colleagues.					
I know how to use powerful questions to get to the heart of an issue.					
I deliver consistent, effective feedback to those around me.					
I regularly ask for feedback on myself.					
I create an environment where all staff feel safe contributing, being themselves, and challenging one another.					
I am confident engaging in difficult conversations when necessary.					
I can create a positive relationship dynamic even within a difficult conversation.					

Sensing the Future Behaviors	Never	Rarely	Sometimes	Frequently	Very Often
I slow down enough to see the big picture.					
I constantly strive for improvement in a way that creates real impact.					
I am curious and invest time in understanding more, often seeking out how others might view the same issue.					
I have the courage to act on ideas and create experiments to try out new approaches.					
I persevere with experiments, continually reviewing and seeking the right solution.					
I can find simple solutions to complex problems.					
I nurture a culture of curiosity and experimentation with my team.					

Seizing Momentum Behaviors	Never	Rarely	Sometimes	Frequently	Very Often
I am purposeful and know the kind of impact I want to have.					
I understand that attention is the key to getting things done.					
I feel in control of my time and how I choose to spend it.					
I prioritize the most important tasks first, rather than just the "quick wins."					
I understand why I procrastinate and know how to avoid it.					
I stay focused on the bigger goal, despite setbacks, and I never give up.					
I can focus on outcomes—not the process.					

Your Presence Behaviors	Never	Rarely	Sometimes	Frequently	Very Often
I am aware of my emotional state and how it affects my leadership.					
I can deliberately manage my state and choose how I respond to challenges.					
I recognize when I am not at my best and the impact it has on me, others, and my work.					
I am confident in my leadership capabilities.					
I feel comfortable being myself in my leadership role.					
I know my native genius and can leverage it in how I lead.					
I am intellectually curious.					

Reflection Questions

1. In which of the MESSY areas do you feel strongest?
2. Which of the MESSY areas do you feel most compelled to develop and grow?
3. Reread the chapter about the area you identified for improvement. Which of the go do actions will you integrate into your everyday practice?

Appendix B

Breakthrough Thinking Guide

Core Skill	Trap	Language	Strategies
Challenging the Status Quo *(looking up)*	Reasonableness Trap *Most problems are not new. Things have been tried before, so there is a reasonable explanation for why they are the way they are.*	• How might we . . . ? • What can we do to . . . ?	Frame Your Issue *What are we trying to solve? Who is it important to? How can we turn it into an inquiry question?*
Inquiring *(looking out)*	Pragmatist Trap *Many leaders are busy and have a pretty good idea of what is going on, so they don't seek out data.*	• What is your experience with . . . ? • Tell me more about . . . • What are your views on . . . ?	Assumptions, Experiences, and Frustrations *Talk to people, learn from their experience, and unearth frustrations.*
Analyzing *(looking down)*	Solution Trap *Many people find it easy to jump from data to solution. They are seduced for a solution too soon.*	• What impact does X have on Y? • So, if we follow this through . . .	Find the Root Cause; Why, Why, Why? *Dig underneath all the factors you have identified and pick out one or two root causes.*

Core Skill	Trap	Language	Strategies
Solving *(looking forward)*	Perfectionist Trap *Perfectionism kicks in, and people let the many failings and inadequacies of their preferred solution dominate.*	• Let's try . . . • How about we . . . • I propose we . . .	Bop It! *Challenge the rules and play with them.*
Persevering *(looking in)*	Achievement Trap *If the goal is really stretching, leaders feel as if they are likely to fail partially or wholly, which can make it tempting to change direction or water down their ambition.*	• What can we learn from . . . ? • How can we overcome this? • Let's not lose sight of what we are aiming for.	Fast-Cycle Experiments *What is the fastest way to test an idea? What can you learn?* Maintaining High Expectations *Keep your focus on the learning and growth; outcomes will follow.*

Appendix C

Four Faces of Coaching Questionnaire

Complete the questionnaire, picking two or three areas you would particularly like to improve.

For each question, check the appropriate box:
• Very Strong: This is an area of outstanding strength. • Strong: This is an area of strength for you in your current role. • Could Develop: This is an area you feel you could do more in. • Must Develop: This is an area that it is important for you to improve.

Challenger	Very Strong	Strong	Could Develop	Must Develop
I challenge poor performance quickly and effectively.				
I find it easy to give negative feedback.				
I encourage people to break the mold and attempt the radical.				
I help people see exactly where they can improve and excite them with the possibility of doing so.				
I challenge people's thinking and help them see bigger possibilities.				
I hold a mirror up to people, helping them see their blind spots (positive or negative).				

Explorer	Very Strong	Strong	Could Develop	Must Develop
People come to me to talk through difficult or personal issues.				
I am comfortable when others express emotion.				
I am a good listener.				
I take time to help others develop their own solutions.				
I am good at getting under the surface of an issue and getting to the heart of what is wrong.				
By taking a step back, I help people look at an old problem in a new way.				
I am good at sharing new ideas and learning.				

Expert	Very Strong	Strong	Could Develop	Must Develop
I am respected and seen as a role model by my team.				
I set high standards.				
When appropriate, I tell people exactly what to do in a given situation.				
I do things others try to emulate and learn from.				
I am regularly sought out for advice on a host of issues.				
I make time to share my experience and knowledge with my team.				
I explain things in a clear and compelling way.				
I make the time to show people how to do things in a thorough and complete way.				

Supporter	Very Strong	Strong	Could Develop	Must Develop
I build the confidence of those around me.				
I find it easy to give praise.				
I find it easy to see the best in people (and spot their potential).				
I find stretching tasks for my people to do, giving them the opportunity to grow.				
I empower my team, helping them find their own solutions to problems (rather than doing it for them).				

References

Asplund, J., & Blacksmith, N. (2011). The secret of higher performance: How integrating employee engagement and strengths boosts both. *Gallup.* https://news.gallup.com/businessjournal/147383/secret-higher-performance.aspx

Assagioli, R. (2007). *Transpersonal development.* Smiling Wisdom.

Brown, B. (2010, June). The power of vulnerability [Video]. TED Conferences. www.ted.com/talks/brene_brown_the_power_of_vulnerability

Brown, B. (2013). *The power of vulnerability: Teachings on authenticity, connection, and courage.* Sounds True.

Brown, B. (2018). *Dare to lead: Brave work. Tough conversations. Whole hearts.* Random House.

Connor, J., & Hirani, K. (2019). *The four greatest coaching conversations: Change mindsets, shift attitudes, and achieve extraordinary results.* Nicholas Brealey.

Connor, J., Parisi, J., & Peskett, S. (2020). The uncommon sense of MESSY leadership. https://bts.com/insights/the-uncommon-sense-of-messy-leadership-2

Covey, S. R. (n.d.). Big rocks [Video]. FranklinCovey. https://resources.franklincovey.com/the-8th-habit/big-rocks-stephen-r-covey

Covey, S. R. (2013). *The 7 habits of highly effective people: Powerful lessons in personal change.* Simon & Schuster.

Curtiss, P. R., & Warren, P. W. (1973). *The dynamics of life skills coaching. Life skills series.* Saskatchewan NewStart.

Day, C., Sammons, P., & Gorgen, K. (2016). *Successful school leadership.* Education Development Trust.

de Bono, E. (1993). *Serious creativity: Using the power of lateral thinking to create new ideas.* HarperCollins.

DeWitt, P. (2016). *Collaborative leadership: Six influences that matter most.* Corwin.

DeWitt, P. (2021). Educators, it's time to 'declutter' your practice. *EdWeek.* https://www.edweek.org/leadership/opinion-if-youre-only-focusing-on-deep-breathing-in-school-you-dont-understand-the-problem/2021/09

Dilts, R. (1990). *Changing belief systems with NLP.* Meta Publications.

Drucker, P. F. (2006). *Classic Drucker: Essential wisdom of Peter Drucker from the pages of* Harvard Business Review. Harvard Business School Press.

Duckworth, A. (2016). *Grit: Why passion and persistence are the secrets to success.* Penguin.

Edmondson, A. (1999). Psychological safety and learning behavior in work teams. *Administrative Science Quarterly, 44*(2), 350–383.

Fritz, R. (2014). *The path of least resistance: Learning to become the creative force in your own life.* Butterworth-Heinemann.

Fullan, M. (2018). *Nuance: Why some leaders succeed and others fail.* Corwin.

Geraskov, E. A. (1994). The internal contradiction and the unconscious sources of activity. *Journal of Psychology, 128*(6), 625–634.

Goldhaber, D., Krieg, J., Naito, N., & Theobald, R. (2020). Making the most of student teaching: The importance of mentors and scope for change. *Education Finance and Policy, 15*(3), 581–591.

Grissom, J. A., Egalite, A. J., & Lindsay, C. A. (2021). *How principals affect students and schools.* Wallace Foundation.

Hannon, V., & Mackay, A. (2021). *The future of educational leadership: Five signposts.* Centre for Strategic Education. https://ncee.org/quick-read/the-future-of-educational-leadership-five-signposts

Hattie, J. (2008). *Visible learning: A synthesis of over 800 meta-analyses relating to achievement.* Routledge.

Hattie, J., & Zieler, K. (2017). *Ten mindframes for visible learning.* Corwin.

Heen, S., & Stone, D. (2014). Find the coaching in criticism. *Harvard Business Review.* https://hbr.org/2014/01/find-the-coaching-in-criticism

Kaser, L., & Halbert, J. (2009). *Leadership mindsets: Innovation and learning in the transformation of schools.* Routledge.

Kelley, D., & Kelley, T. (2013). *Creative confidence: Unleashing the creative potential within us all.* Crown Business.

Kondo, M. (2014). *The life-changing magic of tidying up: The Japanese art of decluttering and organizing.* Ten Speed Press.

Kraft, M. A., Blazar, D., & Hogan, D. (2018). The effect of teacher coaching on instruction and achievement: A meta-analysis of the causal evidence. *Review of Educational Research, 88*(4), 547–588.

Leithwood, K. (2012). *Strong districts and their leadership.* Council of Ontario Directors of Education.

Leithwood, K., Harris, A., & Hopkins, D. (2008). Seven strong claims about successful school leadership. *School Leadership & Management, 28*(1), 27–42.

Leithwood, K., Harris, A., & Hopkins, D. (2020). Seven strong claims about successful school leadership revisited. *School Leadership & Management, 40*(1), 5–22.

Leithwood, K., & Jantzi, D. (2008). Linking leadership to student learning: The contributions of leader efficacy. *Educational Administration Quarterly, 44,* 496–528.

Matthews, P. (2019). *Incremental coaching in schools.* Ambition School Leadership.

Officevibe. (2022). Statistics on the importance of employee feedback. https://officevibe.com/blog/infographic-employee-feedback

Organisation for Economic Co-operation and Development. (2014). Education at a glance 2014: OECD indicators. https://www.oecd-ilibrary.org/docserver/eag-2014-en.pdf

Pink, D. (2011). *Drive: The surprising truth about what motivates us.* Riverhead.

Robinson, V. (2017). *Capabilities required for leading improvement: Challenges for researchers and developers.* Paper presented at ACER Research Conference 2017.

Sahlberg, P. (2021). A conversation with Pasi Sahlberg on the future of educational leadership. https://www.youtube.com/watch?v=KAWWEIZDpLw

Schmidt, E., Rosenberg, J., & Eagle, A. (2019). *Trillion dollar coach: The leadership playbook of Silicon Valley's Bill Campbell.* Harper Business.

Siegel, D. J. (2021). *The developing mind: How relationships and the brain interact to shape who we are* (3rd ed.). Guilford.

Sinek, S. (2011). *Start with why: How great leaders inspire everyone to take action.* Penguin.

Slade, S., & Gallagher, A. (2022). The world seems complicated: Perhaps it's time to be more human. https://www.edweek.org/leadership/opinion-the-world-seems-complicated-perhaps-its-time-to-be-more-human/2022/11

Tinney, J., & O'Brien, T. (2020). Professional well-being through coaching: Personalized support for school leaders. *EdCan Network Blog*. https://www.edcan.ca/articles/professional-well-being-through-coaching

Watkins, A. (2013). *Coherence: The secret science of brilliant leadership.* Kogan Page.

Wilber, K. (2000). *Integral psychology: Consciousness, spirit, psychology, therapy.* Shambala Publications.

Wiseman, L. (2017). *Multipliers, revised and updated: How the best leaders make everyone smart.* Harper Business.

Zenger, J., & Folkman, J. (2013). The ideal praise-to-criticism ratio. *Harvard Business Review*. https://hbr.org/2013/03/the-ideal-praise-to-criticism

Index

The letter *f* following a page locator denotes a figure.

About the Authors

Alyssa Gallagher co-leads BTS Spark in North America, helping school leaders across the United States and Canada access leadership coaching and professional development. Alyssa combines experience of school leadership and school district administration with expertise in leadership development. She spent 20 years in the U.S. public education K–12 sector, filling many roles, including teacher, principal, and assistant superintendent.

Under Alyssa's guidance, Los Altos School District (California) became a nationally recognized leader in educational innovation, and her work was featured on CNN and by *Forbes, Wired, The Economist,* and *60 Minutes*. She worked with Sal Khan to lead the first ever pilot of Khan Academy in classrooms across an entire school district. Alyssa then served as director of global leadership for the Wiseman Group, guiding leaders to make everyone around them smarter and more capable.

Alyssa has coauthored two books with Kami Thordarson on using design thinking to improve teaching and learning: *Design Thinking for School Leaders: Five Roles and Mindsets That Ignite Positive Change* (2018) and *Design Thinking in Play: An Action Guide for Educators* (2020).

She can be reached at alyssa.gallagher@btsspark.org.

Rosie Connor founded BTS Spark and has led its educational leadership development and coaching work for over a decade. As global director, she has designed and launched hundreds of leadership development programs for school leaders across four continents. Motivated by a passion for supporting school leaders and teachers to do their best work, Rosie brings 25 years of experience in educational leadership.

As chief executive of one of Tony Blair's Education Action Zones, her leadership in turning around 19 failing schools was described by independent inspectors as "outstanding" and was nominated by England's Department for Education as a national flagship. Working with the UK's National College for School Leadership and the Innovation Unit, Rosie advised schools on how to form successful professional learning communities. After emigrating to Australia, she worked with the Australian Institute for Teaching and School Leadership to lead the launch of the national professional standard for school principals.

Rosie was selected as a 2023 Most Influential Educator by Australia's *The Educator* magazine. She collaborates with the World Innovation Summit for Education, OECD2030, and leading-edge school systems on future-focused school leadership post-pandemic. She can be reached at rosie.connor@btsspark.org.

bts spark
school leadership made personal

BTS Spark is a not-for-profit global educational leadership practice, dedicated to supporting school leaders to build their capability to lead their school communities effectively. Its mission is to provide schools with access to world-class leadership coaching and workshops at not-for-profit prices.

BTS Spark collaborates with school systems, school districts, educational leadership institutes, not-for-profit organizations, universities, and schools to unlock the leadership potential of education leaders. Its global team of 300 professional accredited leadership coaches span 37 countries and six continents and are available to support school leaders in 34 world languages.

BTS Spark has developed a comprehensive evidence-based curriculum of 33 leadership mindsets and capabilities that underpin effective school leadership, enabling professional development to be targeted at different levels of education leaders and personalized to individuals' needs.

BTS Spark is the social impact arm of BTS, a multi-award-winning global leadership consultancy. BTS Spark collaborates with OECD2030, World Innovation Summit for Education (WISE), Global Education Leaders' Partnership (GELP), UNESCO, and progressive school systems worldwide.

To find out more about BTS Spark's MESSY leadership and coaching programs, contact hello@btsspark.org or browse the website at https://btsspark.org.

Related ASCD Resources: School Leadership

At the time of publication, the following resources were available (ASCD stock numbers in parentheses).

Design Thinking for School Leaders: Five Roles and Mindsets That Ignite Positive Change by Alyssa Gallagher & Kami Thordarson (#118022)

Design Thinking in Play: An Action Guide for Educators by Alyssa Gallagher & Kami Thordarson (#120030)

The EQ Way: How Emotionally Intelligent School Leaders Navigate Turbulent Times by Ignacio Lopez (#123046)

The Principal as Chief Empathy Officer: Creating a Culture Where Everyone Grows by Thomas R. Hoerr (#122030)

Small Shifts, Meaningful Improvement: Collective Leadership Strategies for Schools and Districts by P. Ann Byrd, Alesha Daughtrey, Jonathan Eckert, & Lori Nazareno (#123007)

Stop Leading, Start Building: Turn Your School into a Success Story with the People and Resources You Already Have by Robyn R. Jackson (#121025)

What If I'm Wrong? and Other Key Questions for Decisive School Leadership by Simon Rodberg (#121009)

For up-to-date information about ASCD resources, go to www.ascd.org. You can search the complete archives of *Educational Leadership* at www.ascd.org/el. To contact us, sent an email to member@ascd.org or call 800-933-2723 or 703-578-9600.

ascd
whole child

The ASCD Whole Child approach is an effort to transition from a focus on narrowly defined academic achievement to one that promotes the long-term development and success of all children. Through this approach, ASCD supports educators, families, community members, and policymakers as they move from a vision about educating the whole child to sustainable, collaborative actions.

Embracing MESSY Leadership relates to the **safe** and **supported** tenets.
For more about the ASCD Whole Child approach, visit ***www.ascd.org/wholechild.***

WHOLE CHILD TENETS

1 **HEALTHY**
Each student enters school healthy and learns about and practices a healthy lifestyle.

2 **SAFE**
Each student learns in an environment that is physically and emotionally safe for students and adults.

3 **ENGAGED**
Each student is actively engaged in learning and is connected to the school and broader community.

4 **SUPPORTED**
Each student has access to personalized learning and is supported by qualified, caring adults.

5 **CHALLENGED**
Each student is challenged academically and prepared for success in college or further study and for employment and participation in a global environment.

Become an ASCD member today!
Go to www.ascd.org/joinascd
or call toll-free: 800-933-ASCD (2723)

ascd

DON'T MISS A SINGLE ISSUE OF ASCD'S AWARD-WINNING MAGAZINE.

ascd
educational
leadership

If you belong to a Professional Learning Community, you may be looking for a way to get your fellow educators' minds around a complex topic. Why not delve into a relevant theme issue of *Educational Leadership*, the journal written by educators for educators?

Subscribe now, or purchase back issues of ASCD's flagship publication at **www.ascd.org/el**. Discounts on bulk purchases are available.

To see more details about these and other popular issues of *Educational Leadership*, visit **www.ascd.org/el/all**.

ascd®
2800 Shirlington Road
Suite 1001
Arlington, VA 22206 USA

www.ascd.org/learnmore